# The Art of
# Cartooning Anything

## HIMANSHU MIRE
Animator, Illustrator, Programmer & Teacher

**BLUEROSE PUBLISHERS**
India | U.K.

Copyright © Himanshu Mire 2025

All rights reserved by author. No part of this publication may be reproduced, stored in a retrieval system or transmitted in any form or by any means, electronic, mechanical, photocopying, recording or otherwise, without the prior permission of the author. Although every precaution has been taken to verify the accuracy of the information contained herein, the publisher assumes no responsibility for any errors or omissions. No liability is assumed for damages that may result from the use of information contained within.

BlueRose Publishers takes no responsibility for any damages, losses, or liabilities that may arise from the use or misuse of the information, products, or services provided in this publication.

For permissions requests or inquiries regarding this publication, please contact:

BLUEROSE PUBLISHERS
www.BlueRoseONE.com
info@bluerosepublishers.com
+91 8882 898 898
+4407342408967

ISBN: 978-93-7018-240-0

First Edition: February 2025

# CONTENT

## Introduction

# CHAPTER -1
## Shape & Character Design

### Basic shapes

- Line and types of lines & practice exercise
- Geometric shapes
- Freeform & natural form shapes
- Merging shapes
- Make face using basic shapes
- Simple shapes to form face variation
- Same shapes but different variations

### Hands

- Hand construction
- Variation in Hands
- Fingers
- Types of fingers

### Legs

- Legs Construction
- Types of cartoon legs
- Shoes and sendels

## Facial feature
- Ears and their variation
- Mouth
- Hair for male and female
- Beards

## Clothing
- Male
- Female
- Clothing Style

## Drawing in 3D
- Face turn around
- Draw from reference
- Perspective for characters

## Cute character
- Exaggerated Features
- Unique Traits

## Draw non-living things
- Smoke
- Fire
- Water
- Paper & leaf
- Breakdown real-life things into drawings

## Silhouettes
- Proportions
- Negative Space
- Audience
- Focus on Form
- Simplicity and Clarity
- Emotional Impact

# CHAPTER - 2
## The Art of Expression

### Expressions

- Emotions sheets
- Body language and line of actions
- Emotional Tone
- Make your own IP
- Keywords for design

# CHAPTER - 3
## Visual Design

### Fundementals

- One-Point Perspective
- Two-Point Perspective:
- Three-Point Perspective
- Multi-Point Perspective

### Horizontals

- Markers (bulid the gemotary) technic
- Selling points
- Forms & Grids
- Establishing shots
- Camera
- Environment setup (fore ground , middle ground & background)
- Design formula
- Camera
- Detail distribution
- Entertainment design
- Thumbnil design

- Mixing design
- Visual memory
- References

## Composition

- Environment + interior design
- The rule of third & golden ration
- Dynamic composition
- Set design
- Mixing design

# CHAPTER -4
## Colour Principles

### Colour theory

- Colour theory fundamental
- Colour knowledge
- values
- Colour balance
- Balance composition
- Lights reflection & atmosphere
- Lighting and values
- Colour pallets & mood
- Stage character
- Approaching a scene
- Page balance and presentation
- Apply colour to the characters

# CHAPTER -5
## Design Strategy

### General Tips

- Freelance Tips
- Portfolio
- Design solution for business
- Pipeline
- Things to avoid
- Clients need and clients want !
- Grow your money Mindset.

- Thanks
- About Author

# INTRODUCTION

This book aims to bridge that gap by teaching you how to leverage your artistic skills to create characters and environments that not only engage but also have commercial potential. To make a cartoon character that has a unique identity? Using knowledge of this book you Can easily convey to your audience from all age groups that this cartoon character exists. There are various books available on the market on illustration, color theory, Art fundamentals in your drawing, etc. but only a few focus on the intersection of art and business.

In this book, we will explore both the art of drawing and the business of creating characters. We'll discuss how to create drawings that effectively represent what the character is thinking and feeling. Throughout this process, I will teach you the essential craft knowledge needed for success. The content will be divided into five chapters. In the first chapter, we will cover how to use basic shapes to define your character. In the second chapter, we will discuss how to bring expression to these shapes, making them feel alive. In the third chapter, we will focus on using fundamental principles and composition to make your art stand out.

In the fourth chapter, we will explore color theory and how it can influence our psychology and emotions. In the final chapter, we will learn how to apply our knowledge and passion to make money. Remember, there are countless ways to approach art, and this book presents one effective method. Art is a universal language. I wrote this book with the hope that it will inspire and transform lives. If someone's life is changed by reading and practicing this book, that will be the greatest reward for me!

*Himanshu Mire*

## CONCEPTION

YOU ARE A ARTIST ON A ADVENTURE

# C-1 Fundamentals of Shape & Character Design

## Basic shapes

In this chapter, we will learn how basic shapes are used to develop the geometry of a character. Basic shapes are the fundamental drawing forms that define the overall structure and proportions of the character.

**EVERYTHING IN DRAWING MADEUP OF SIMPLE SHAPES**

## Geometric Shapes

Geometric shapes are specific shapes made up of lines, curves, and points. They are also known as structural shapes.

Geometric shapes keep drawings simple and easy to understand, helping the audience to quickly and effectively convey the message.

Note: A character becomes richer when you define it for the audience.

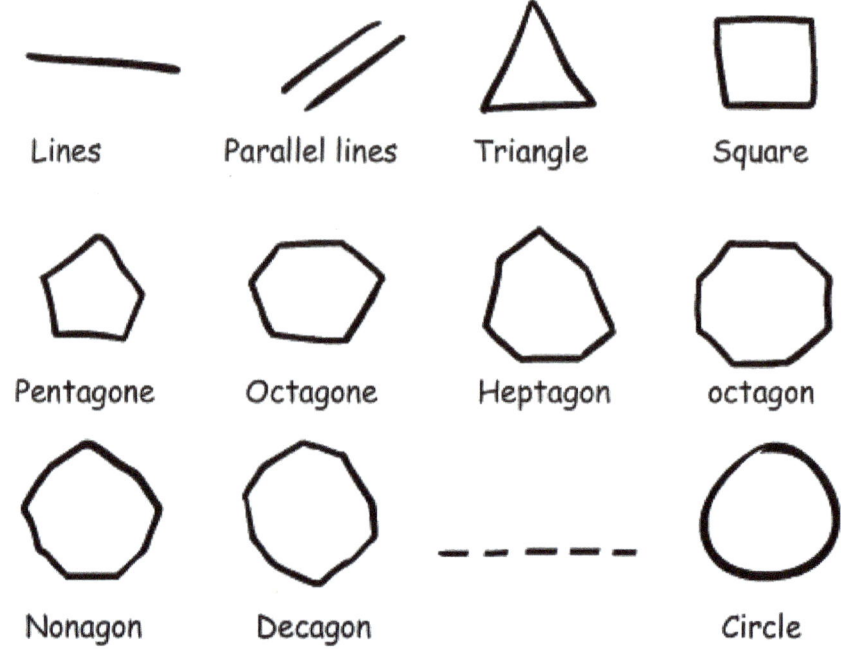

When you are creating shapes, make shapes that communicate proportion and help define your character. At the initial stage, focus on creating communication drawings.

## IN DESIGN THERE ARE 3 BASIC SHAPES MOSTLY USE

Here are some basic shapes, each representing a different personality each basic shape symbolizes a unique personality trait, with distinct characteristics that convey various emotional or behavioral qualities.

The most important shapes are the circle, triangle, and square, and most early traditional cartoon character constructions were created using circles.

If your drawing skills are not strong, start with a circle, as it is easy to manipulate.

## Freeform shapes

Freeform shapes are irregular shapes. Their outlines may be curved, angular, or a combination of both. Examples include a leaf, paper, etc.

## Merging Shapes

If you are merging several shapes together, make sure the overall design has a unique look. Here are some examples.

# LINE AND TYPE OF LINES

## Lines

Lines can be combined to form geometric or organic shapes. They are used to create shapes, define forms, and convey movement.

There are various types of lines, such as:

**1. Vertical Lines** - Lines that run up and down convey strength and stability.

*Vertical Lines*

**2. Horizontal Lines** - Lines that run side to side represent calmness and tranquility.

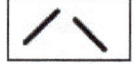

*Horizontal Lines*

**3. Diagonal Lines** - Lines that slant at an angle represent movement, dynamism, or tension.

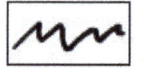

*Diagonal Lines*

**4. Zig-Zag Lines** - Composed of segments rather than being continuous, this represents movement or interruption.

*Zig-Zag Lines*    This can create scene of Excitement or chaos.

**5. Counter Lines** - These lines define the edges and surfaces of objects and help create the illusion of three-dimensionality.

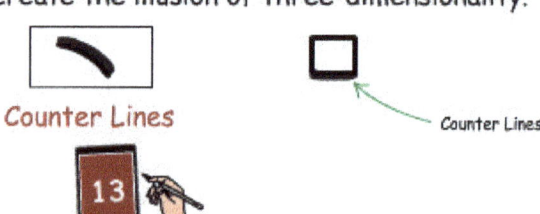

*Counter Lines*        *Counter Lines*

6. **Curved Lines** - These are flowing lines that represent a sense of grace or softness..

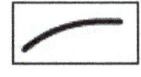

Curved Lines

Lines enhance the artist's drawings and help communicate ideas and emotions.

## Practice #1

If you have never drawn before, here is a small exercise for you.

EXERCISE - Pick up a piece of paper and make dots on both sides. the goal is to draw each line in a single stroke.

Draw as many as you can. This will improve your hand skills.

## Practice #2

After you are done with this, make random dots on the paper and connect them in a single stroke.

Random Dots          Connected Dots

Try this exercise with different shapes, but when making a circle, try to draw it in a single, continuous round.

## Make Face Using Basic Shapes

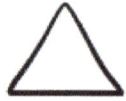  

Step-1) Add basic shapes.

Step-2) Once you have added the basic shapes, try to modify them. Define geometry and basic construction lines.

Step-3) Now, add expression and secondary details on top (you will learn more about expression in Chapter 2).

## 3D SHAPES

There are three basic shapes: square, triangle, and circle. Use these three basic shapes to create different types of shapes with varying geometric proportions and angles.

For Three-dimensional objects, try to create a cube, sphere, cone, and cylinder.

sphere        Cone         Cube

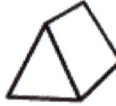  

Triangular prism    Cylinder      Cuboid

Many things we draw in cartoons are three-dimensional.

## Face Shape Variations

Now, we are using common emotions and applying them to different shapes.

## Same Shapes but different Variations

Now, we are using the same shapes and applying different emotions to them.

## Basic Steps to Create a Face

Step-1) Choose basic shapes these serve as the foundation for your character. (Sketch the base shapes lightly.)

Step-2) Define facial features – experiment with the shapes of the eyes, mouth, and nose.

Step-3) Add accessories include items that match the character's personality, such as hats, glasses, clothing, earrings, etc.

Step-4) Add defined colors use different colors to define the character.

REMEMBER :- BRIGHT COLORS CAN CONVEY A CHEERFUL CHARACTER, WHILE MUTED TONES MIGHT SUGGEST A MORE SERIOUS MOOD. AND DARK COLORS CAN CONVEY SADNESS OR POVERTY.

Step-5) Expressions - Draw multiple facial expressions (happy, sad, angry, surprised) using the same base shapes.

Tip: Alter the eyebrows and mouth to convey different emotions.

## HANDS

Most beginner artists struggle when drawing hands. Drawing hands can be fun. There are many ways and styles to draw hands, such as Tom & Jerry-style hands, comic book cartoon hands, anime-style hands, and much more.

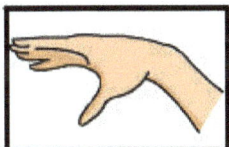

Cartoon Hands     Anime Hands     Comic Hands

Cartoon hand drawings are just exaggerations of reality. Some cartoon characters have three fingers, while others have four. Typically, their cartoon drawings feature three or four fingers. The style of the character can affect the drawing, but in cartoon art, we focus on simplifying details and emphasizing gestures.

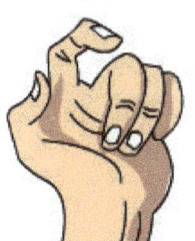

### Details Cartoon Hand Drawing

Using clean, bold lines to define shapes and forms, which is characteristic of cartoon art. Applying vibrant colors to enhance visual appeal and convey emotions or themes. Capturing dynamic poses and facial expressions to bring characters to life and communicate their feelings. You can try three or four fingers to see which looks better for your character. Cartoon hands can be bent, stretched, squashed, twisted, and distorted.

The middle finger should be taller.

Fingers are attached to the corners.

The thumb always extends out from the bottom line.

This line should not be straight.

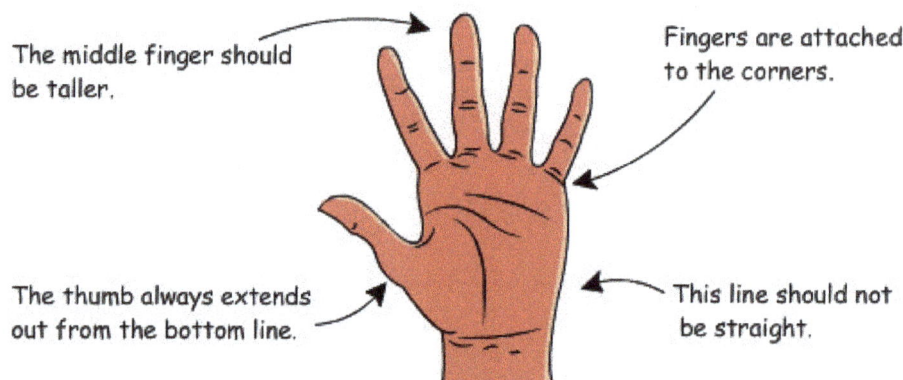

These are the basic shapes of a hand.

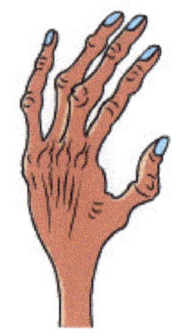

Cartoon hands are more exaggerated than real hands, which creates a distinct art style.

If you're drawing the back of the hand, don't forget to add the knuckles.

Comic and manga hands don't involve much exaggeration their style is similar to real hands.

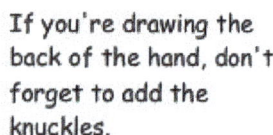

Place the knuckles according to perspective, and position the nails at the corners, not in the middle.

Don't panic when you see this art style. With patience and practice, you can improve your drawings.

## There are four Rules of hand drawing.

STEP-1) Start with basic shapes, whether it's a square, triangle, or circle.

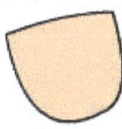  

STEP-2) Add lines to these shapes These lines represent the joints of the palms.

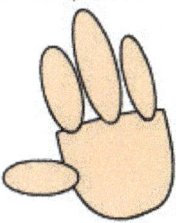  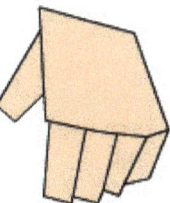

STEP-3) Use basic anatomy knowledge to make the fingers smaller than the palm, not larger.

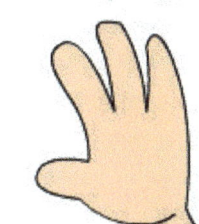 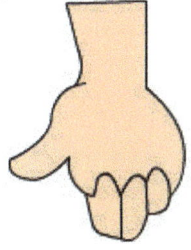 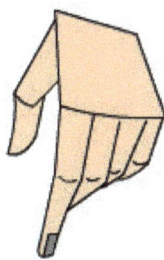

STEP-4) Add additional or secondary details, such as wrinkles (for comic style) and fingernails.

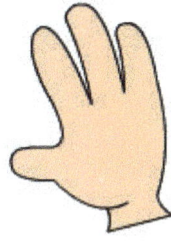 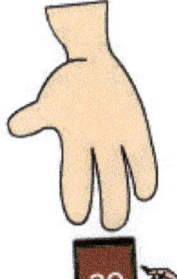 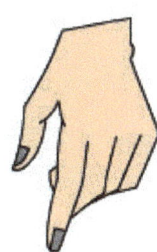

## 3 FINGERS CARTOON HANDS DRAWINGS

Stylization: The use of three fingers is a common stylistic choice in many classic cartoons, such as those from Disney and Looney Tunes. This technique emphasizes a cartoonish look, enhancing the characters exaggerated expressions and actions.

Characters with three fingers often have a more simplified design, making them easier to draw and animate, especially in styles that emphasize quick, expressive movements.

## 4 FINGERS CARTOON HANDS DRAWINGS

Realism: Characters with four fingers tend to appear slightly more realistic while still maintaining a cartoonish style. This balance makes them relatable while preserving their stylized nature Some characters may be designed with four fingers to distinguish them from others or to reflect a specific cultural or artistic influence.

The choice between three-finger and four-finger cartoon hands depends on the artist's style, the intended audience, and the overall design goals of the character. Both approaches have their merits and can effectively convey personality and emotion in different ways.

## Arm Constructions

Before drawing a cartoon arm, it's essential to understand its anatomy and muscle placement to ensure the cartoon version mirrors real-life proportions.

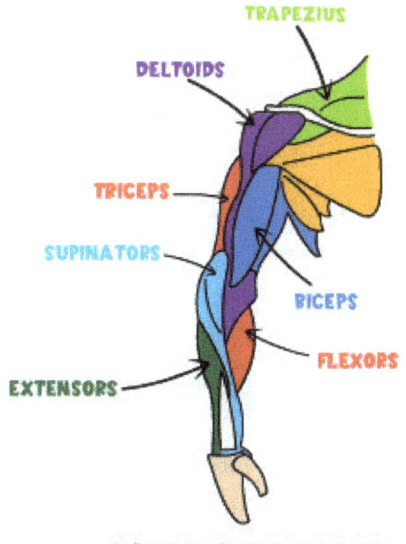

**ARMS ANATOMY**

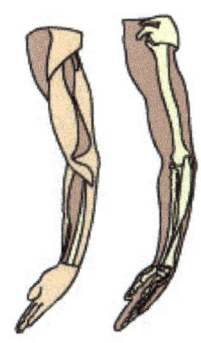

**STRUCTURE ARMS**

Structure arms focus on building a framework to establish proportion, form, and position, helping artists understand how the arm parts relate within the overall pose.

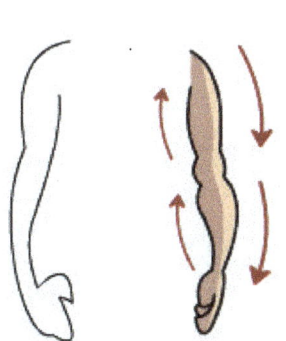

**GESTURE ARMS**

Gesture arms capture movement and energy, essential in gesture drawing, which involves quick, loose sketches that express the human form's action and fluidity.

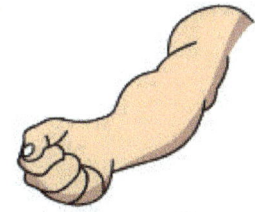

**DYNAMIC ARMS**

These arms are typically exaggerated to emphasize the motion, making the character appear more lively and expressive. Dynamic arms are often used in cartoons to convey emotion, power, or excitement.

## Balance the character

Once you design the arms and legs, you must balance the character's overall geometry; otherwise, the proportions may look off, and the audience may have difficulty relating to the character.

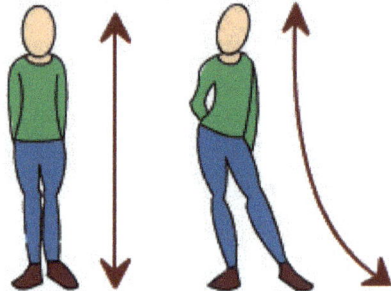

**POSE BALANCE**

Balancing a cartoon character involves physical aspects to create a design that feels stable and believable.

Both legs should have consistent proportions and structure, ensuring balance, natural appearance, and believability in the character's design.

**CONSISTENT LEG PROPORTIONS**

**LEGS SHOULD BALANCE BODY**

The legs should have proper proportions and positioning in relation to the rest of the character's body If the character is wearing shorts or pants, their legs should be designed to support the character's weight and balance, and they should fit the overall context of the scene.

## Type of Arms

(1) Simplified Arms - Design uses basic shapes and exaggerated proportions to create a clean, stylized look. Common in cartoons and animation, it enhances expressiveness while making characters easy to draw and visually appealing.

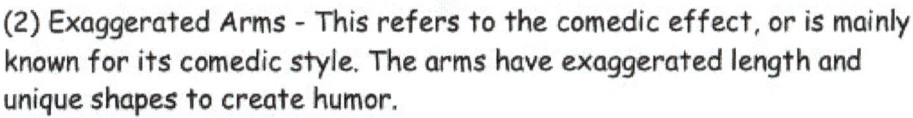

(2) Exaggerated Arms - This refers to the comedic effect, or is mainly known for its comedic style. The arms have exaggerated length and unique shapes to create humor.

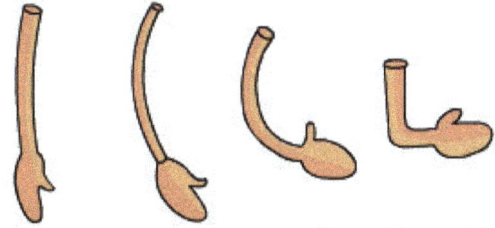

(3) Power Action poses - These arms are primarily used in action scenes, representing moments with multiple hands and the energy of the arms. They are used to convey motion and excitement.

Tips - Learn in baby steps

**THIS DEALS WITH THE DYNAMIC POSES.**

This are Different drawing styles pick one that work best for you cartoons, observation of real life arm movement and exgurate them will improve your skill in arm drawing and later you develop your own art style.

# Fingers

The construction of cartoon fingers is often done in exaggerated forms or segmented shapes. For a super-cartoonish look, divide each finger into two or three parts using curved lines to represent the flow of energy. Break things down into simple forms so they appear more interesting.

## HANDS ARE A LITTLE BIT CHALLENGING.

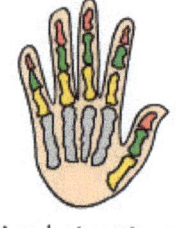 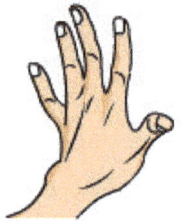 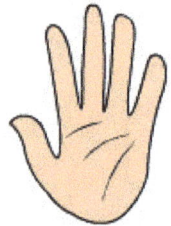

Hand structues         Back side         Front side

Remember - Fingers are tricky things specially when you animate things later.

The way fingers are designed or structured in a balanced manner, with space and proportions divided equally."

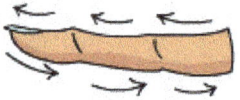

50-50 space distribution

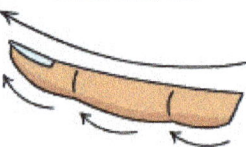

Fingers are flexible so make them in form of arc.

The L-shape creates dynamic motion and expression, giving designs an energetic, exaggerated look that emphasizes movement and action.

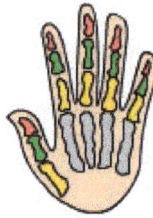

Wifi principal Arc Rythum

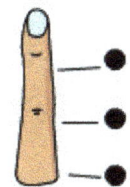

Hands Energy Flow

For realistic proportions, observe your own hands or reference images, then stylize them from there.

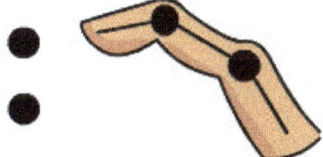

Press and Press out the them so it look real

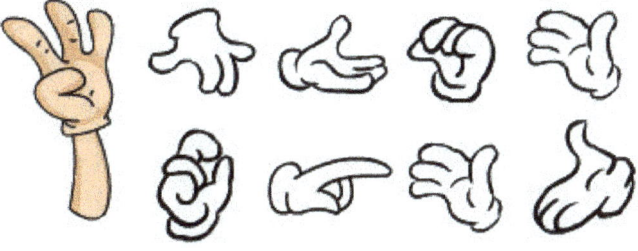

Finger drawings are formed using basic shapes, and you should ensure an equal distribution of lines.

**HIGHLY STYLE CARTOONY HAND MICKY MOUSE HANDS**

Here are some practical exercises to help you draw hands more easily and effectively:
Start by picking a shape, then sketch and define the dimensions or shape of the palm. Commonly used shapes include oval, rectangle, and circle. For the fingers, use small, simple lines and connect them. This will give the fingers shape and make them slightly tapered at the tips.

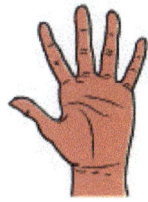

Whenever you are animating or designing the same character's hand multiple times, make sure there is an equal distribution of lines in your character.

## Types of Fingers

Just like hands, fingers are also categorized into various styles, such as:-

(1) Micky mouse fingers
(2) Comic fingers
(3) stylised hands
(4) simple fingers

Stylization - make the fingers thicker or thinner than they would be in reality to create a more exaggerated look.

Details - To add details, draw simple rectangles, squares, or ovals for the nails. These can be small ovals or triangles, depending on your personal choice.

Positioning - Positioning is one of the most important elements for adding style, especially in illustration, to create perspective. The appearance of objects changes slightly when drawn from different angles. Adjust the size and shape of the fingers accordingly.

Almost all man-made objects consist of symmetrical.

Dynamic look - Once your sketch is complete, add a darker outline, apply colors to the fingers, and add shading for highlights. This will create depth.

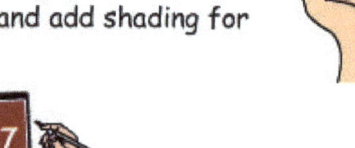

## REMEMBER

In the beginning stages, finding your unique style can be challenging, but it's a normal part of the process. Developing your personal style takes time, practice, and experimentation. Experiment with different techniques, forms, and subjects to discover what resonates with you.
Stay open to learning from others while maintaining your individuality. Continuously explore new ideas, even if they differ from your usual approach. Embrace change and growth, as this will refine your style and strengthen your artistic identity. By diversifying your approach, you'll gain a competitive advantage and advance your career. Take risks and learn from mistakes—they contribute to your success.

# LEGS

To draw a leg, whether for a realistic or stylized figure, it's important to understand the basic bone structure of the human body or have a mental image of it. With this knowledge, you can easily draw the leg.

## UNDERSTAND THE BASIC STRUCTURE

Pelvis - The pelvis supports the upper body when sitting, standing, or walking.

Femur - The femur is your thigh bone. It is the longest and strongest bone in your body, playing a crucial role in your ability to stand and move.

Tibia - The tibia is the second-longest bone in the body and connects to both the knee and ankle joints.

Fibula - It's the smaller of the two bones in your lower leg. It provides structure to your calf and forms the top of your ankle.

Patella - It's the largest bone in your body, protecting the knee joint and helping the quadriceps muscle move the leg.

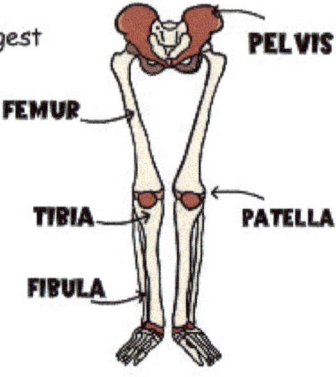

**STATIC BONES POSES**

Diagonal lines represent the dynamic angles of the leg, especially in motion or when showing depth. They help convey movement and the three-dimensional positioning of the bones, making the leg appear more lifelike and dynamic in illustrations or anatomical studies.

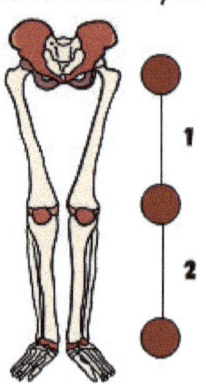

Start with two horizontal lines; this will help you easily understand how long or short your character is

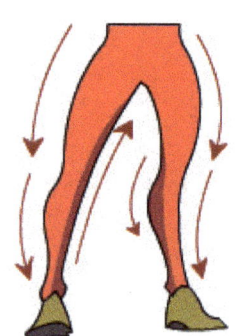

There is differences in the construction of female and male legs. Female legs often exhibit more curves, whereas male legs tend to have a straighter appearance.

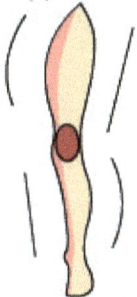 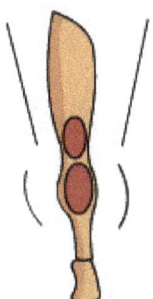

**Female body legs**     **Male body Legs**

Before start with legs first messure the whole body.

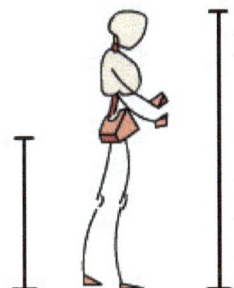

For initial rough work focused on the basic structure, rather than final details.

On the front inner side of the leg, there is a line, while the outer side consists of two curves. You can divide the leg's size just below the knee.

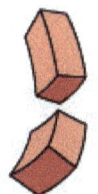

Practice in the form of cubes to eliminate your fear.

Learn to Balance the centre of gravity of the creature.

Just imagine all the object are present in 3D space.

The basic shapes are in place, refine the outline. Add muscle definition, curves, and the contours of the leg.

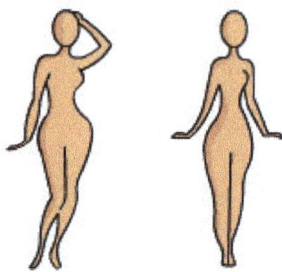

Full front view.

## DESIGN USING LINE OF ACTION

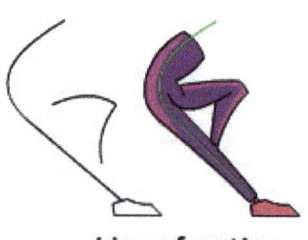

Line of action

Line of action establishing a dynamic, flowing line that represents the primary movement or direction of the figure's body.

## DESIGN USING DIFFERENT ANGLES

Geometric shapes, varying lines, or combining elements at different angles to create depth, interest, and complexity in the design

First go for basic structure rather than the final details, there are four types of designs available. Using these, you can easily understand how to construct the leg and later add the final details.

## Legs Construction

When it comes to the legs, first think about the style you want to convey and consider your character.

Consider their movements and overall vibe. This foundational step guides choices in shape and posture, ensuring the legs enhance the character's identity and create a cohesive, expressive design.

Remember Different style can reflect cultural background. traditional clothing styles, hairstyles, and even body language can vary significantly between cultures

## Varities of cartoon Legs

1) Straight legs: This style is simple and classic, ideal for conveying a straightforward character.

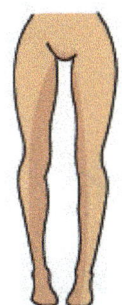

2) Bent legs: Commonly used in action poses or when a character is sitting.

3) Short Legs - This style typically represents cute or chubby characters, as shorter legs can convey a sense of innocence, playfulness, and a more approachable, whimsical appearance

4) Long Legs - This style represents lanky characters, conveying humor and quirkiness, with elongated proportions that enhance their whimsical and playful nature.

 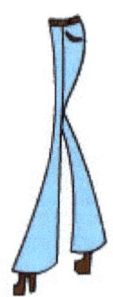 

5) Stylize Legs - Exaggerated proportions, such as very long limbs or tiny feet, create a unique look.

6) Thick Legs - Representing strength and power, this style is commonly used to create muscular characters or gym-goers.

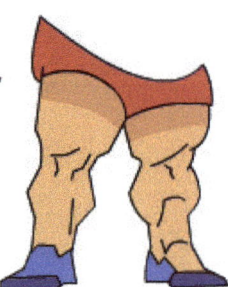

## Shoes and Sendels

### Shoes

### Basic Shape

Start with a simple outline of the shoe. Use basic shapes, like rectangles and ovals, to define the sole and the upper part.

### Sole

Draw the sole as a flat rectangle, adding curves for a more realistic look.

### Upper Part:

Sketch the upper part of the shoe, which can include the tongue, laces, and other design elements. Use curved lines to give it shape.

### Details

Add details such as stitching, laces, eyelets, and any logos or patterns.

### Shading:

Use shading to add depth. Identify a light source and shade the opposite side to create dimension.

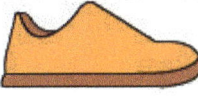

### Final Touches:

Outline your drawing with a darker pencil or pen and erase any unnecessary lines.

# Sendels

  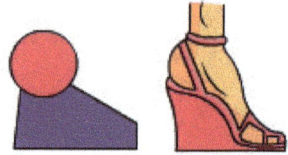

## Basic Shape
Start with the sole, which is usually flatter than that of a shoe. Draw an oval or rectangle for the footbed.

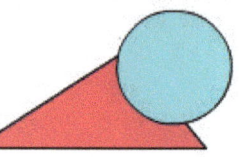

## Straps
Add straps by drawing curved lines that connect to the sole. Think about how they would realistically wrap around the foot.

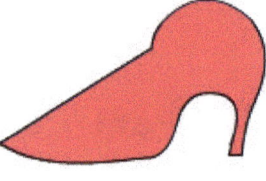

## Details
Include buckles, textures, or patterns on the straps.

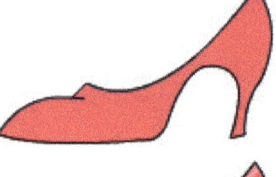

## Shading
As with shoes, add shading to give depth and dimension.

## Final Touches
Clean up your lines and add any final details.

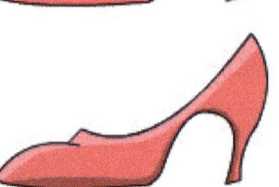

Practice: Don't hesitaqte to try different styles and perspectives.

## Facial Feature
## Ears and their Variation

This sentence suggests that there are many different styles or shapes of ears. By try out. with these variations, you can create a distinctive and individual look for your character.

### (1) Basic Cartoon Ears
This consists of simple rounded or oval shapes, along with basic details represented by simple lines that suggest flow.

### (2) Paint ears
This consists of sharp tops and represents shapes. This is achieved by adding curves and lines to suggest depth and texture.

### (3) Large ears
This has a more exaggerated size, achieved by using outlines and folds for a whimsical effect.

  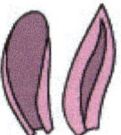

### (4) Tiny Ears
This often used in cute character (baby like characters).

### (5) Stylized Ears
This archive is based on personal choice and has been developed over many experiences. It consists of playing with angles and lines, as well as shading, to create a more artistic look.

# MOUTH

Mouth shapes is essential for accurately expressing emotions in art, animation, or even in real-life interactions. Mouth shapes are mostly consist of expressions. it is crucial for conveing emotions.

Mouth shapes are integral to expressing and interpreting emotions, adding depth to communication.

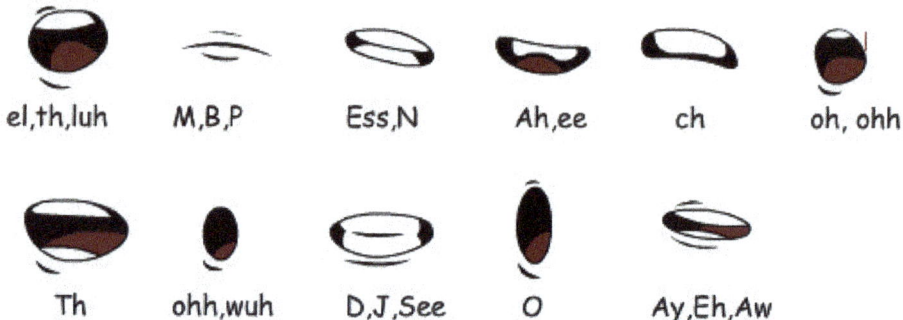

Adding teeth and tongue will enhance the expression especially in open-mouth sceniores.

## TERM TO KNOWN

your mouth style matches the character's overall design and personility and learn how mouth shapes changes with different expressions

## Mouth Variations

(1) Basic mouth - This consists of minimal , may include a straight lines like neutral expressions.

(2) Exaggerated mouth - This represent special emotions & excitements.

(3) small mouth - small simple curved lines & very little details that can convey cutness.

(4) Stylized mouth - This style mostly focus on bold lines and colours for a unique styles.

# PRACTICE

## Male Hair

### HairStyle

Hairstyles for men are determined by various factors, including the shape of the face, hair length, forehead structure, skin tone, and individual preferences. Choosing the right hairstyle can be challenging, but understanding your facial features and comfort level can help guide the decision. Below are some popular hairstyle categories, each with its own distinct appeal and style.

### SHORT HAIRSTYLES

 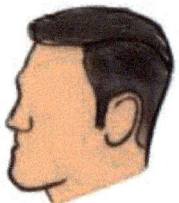  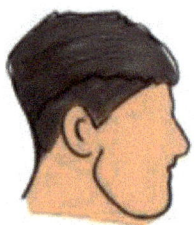

Buzz Cut　　　Crew Cut　　　Ivy League　　　French Crop

### MEDIUM-LENGTH HAIRSTYLES

 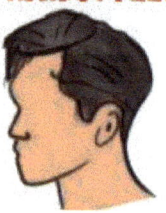 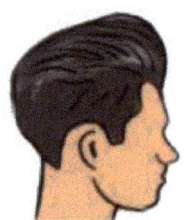 

Textured Crop　　Side Part　　Pompadour　　Quiff

### LONG HAIRSTYLES

Man Bun　　　Ponytail　　　Bro Flow　　　Half-Up, Half-Down

## FADE AND TAPER STYLES

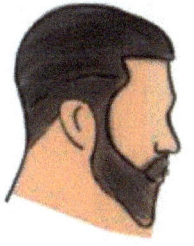 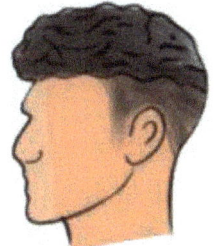 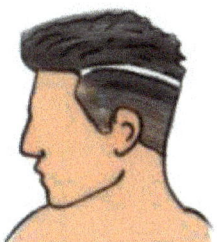 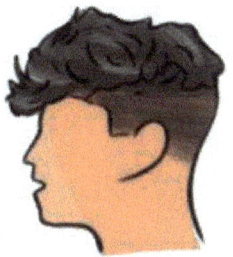

Low Fade    Mid Fade    High Fade    Taper Cut

## UNDERCUT STYLES

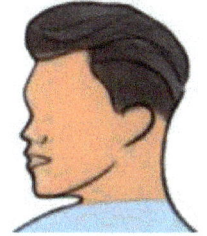 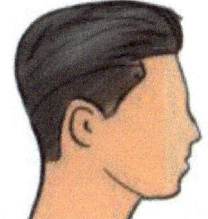 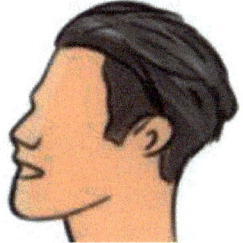

Classic Undercut    Disconnected Undercut    Fade Undercut

## CURLY AND WAVY HAIRSTYLES

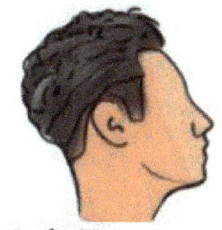  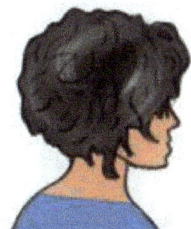

Curly Top    Wavy Fringe    Natural Curls

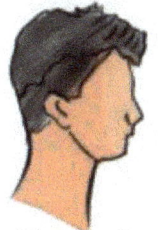   

Mohawk    Faux Hawk    Mullet    Pompadour with Beard

## Male Hair

### Beards

Beard applicable only in adult and old character in cartoon. There are many options available, and choosing the perfect beard can be a bit overwhelming. Whether you're new to growing a beard or just want a fresh look for your character, here are some of the most common types of beards you can choose to design your character and enhance your overall appearance.

| Short Stubble | Long Stubble | Classic Goatee | Van Dyke | Goatee with a Soul Patch | Handlebar Moustache |
|---|---|---|---|---|---|

| Chevron Moustache | Pencil Moustache | Horseshoe Moustache | Short Full Beard | Long Full Beard | Circle Beard |
|---|---|---|---|---|---|

| Anchor Beard | Anchor Beard | Bandholz Beard | Garibaldi Beard | Chinstrap Beard | Balbo Beard |
|---|---|---|---|---|---|

| Soul Patch | Ducktail Beard | Wolverine Beard | | Zappa Beard |
|---|---|---|---|---|

# Female Hairstyle

Female hairstyles can be divided into many types. Here are some common and popular styles that you can use to design your character. Before choosing a character's hairstyle, first determine the character's personality and style.

## Clothing

Once you've decided on your character's shape, it's time to add outfits. However, choosing the right outfit for your character can be a bit tricky and requires careful consideration. In cartoon drawings, there are some key aspects that can help you decide what elements to add to your character in order to achieve an amazing look. Here are 6 keywords that can help you decide your character's personality.

### BACKGROUND

It means to where the character comes from and represents their socio-economic status. For example, a wealthy character might wear designer clothes, while a middle class character would wear simpler clothes.

### PERSONILITY

Clothing should reflect the character's personality, such as bold or adventurous traits. This leads to a personal style, such as casual, formal, traditional, etc.

### BODY TYPE

Character body type represents overall personality and influences their clothing choices as well. For example, a taller character might suit long garments, while a shorter character might look better in more fitted clothes.

### SKINTOONS

Colors can convey emotions, so use color tones that complement the character's features.

### OCCUPATIONS

Character occupations can determine a specific clothing style, such as a chef, soldier, or police officer, etc.

**Character Outfits Based on These Six keywords**

### TIME PEROID & LOCATIONS

The time period also influences clothing style, which changes across different eras: past, present, and future. This can be further categorized into various settings, such as urban, rural, fantasy worlds, or historical contexts, all of which impact clothing choices.

# BASIC SHAPE DRAWINGS BODY TYPE

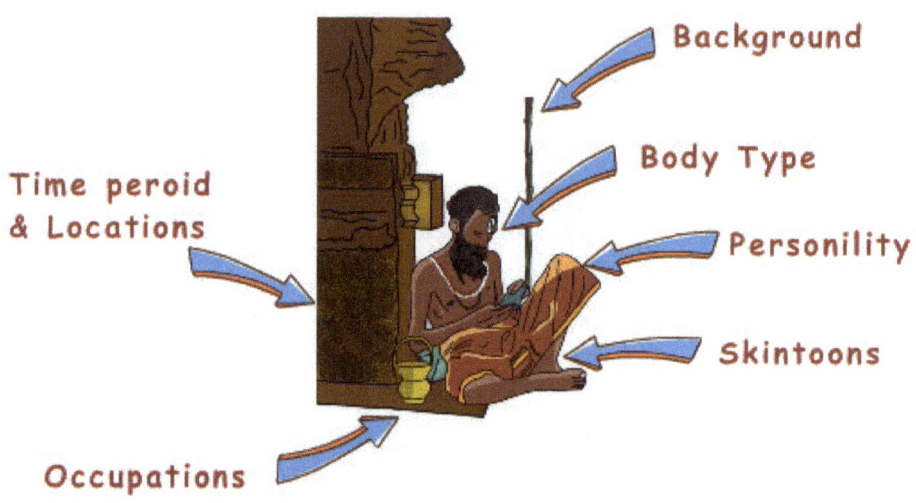

**NOTE :- MOSTLY PRO ARTIST DIRECTLY START WITH CHARACTER CLOTH AND ADD DETAILS LATERS.**

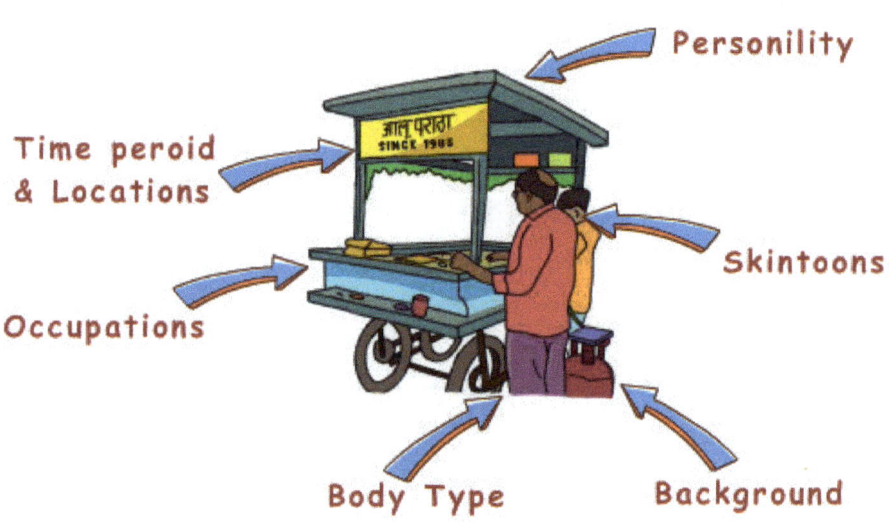

# Male Clothing Style

The most common clothing styles for males that you can use to dress your characters, or you can create numerous permutations and combinations to achieve a unique look for them.

Top wear    +    Bottom wear    =    Outer wear

Begin by learning the various types of clothing available, which will allow you to mix and match pieces creatively. This approach helps in developing a unique, versatile character wardrobe with endless style possibilities.

## FORMAL WEAR

Suits

Dress Shirts

Ties/Bowties

## ATHLETIC WEAR

Gym shorts

Tracksuits

Sneakers

## CASUAL WEAR

T- shirts

Jeans

Shorts

## TRADITIONAL WEAR

  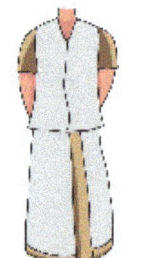 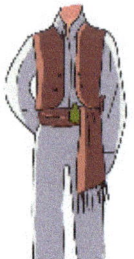

Cultural attire  Kimonos  South Indian  Turkish

## OUTER WEAR

Jackets  Coats  Hoodies

## UNIFORMS WEAR

Labour  Doctor  Manager

## WORK WEAR

Blacksmith  Labour  Hindu Priest

# FEMALE CLOTHING STYLE

There are many types of female dresses, and you can combine any two to create a new look. Here is a collection of dresses you can mix and match to achieve a unique style for your character. You can explore the most common clothing styles for females.

  =

Top Dress  Bottom skirt  Lehenga

## TYPES OF DRESSES

Kurti Styles

Gown Styles

 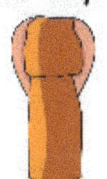 

Sleeveless styles

  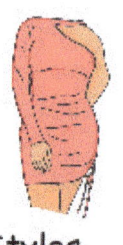 

Bodycon Styles

Misses Styles

Frock Styles

Ball Gown Styles

One-Shoulder Styles

# TYPES TOPS AND TUNICS STYLE

## Long Kurtas Variation

## Blouse Variation

 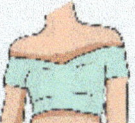   

## T-shirt Variation

# TYPES BOTTOMS STYLE

 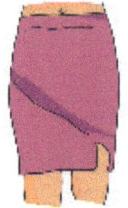 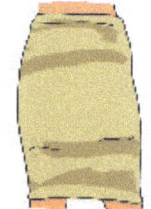

### Bodycon Skirt Variation

### Pleated Skirt Variation

   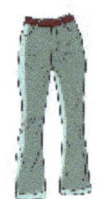 

### Jeans Variation

 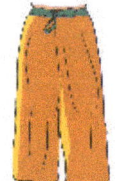 

### Jumpsuit Variation

### Shorts Variation

# TYPES FULL BODY DRESS STYLE

Jumpsuit

Wrap

Salwar suit

Maxi Skirt Variations

Saree Variations

## Drawing in 3D
### Face Turn Around

Face Turnaround involves creating a series of views of the face from different angles while ensuring that the 2D drawings follow a 3D perspective. This approach makes the painting more realistic and believable. By thinking in 3D, you can depict the face from any angle. It helps to visualize the character's face in three dimensions and is often used in character design.

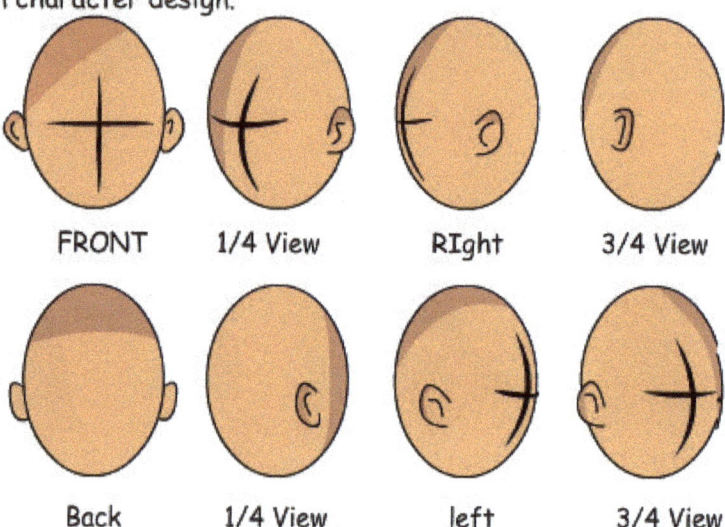

Creating a 3D sketch is helpful because, when working in freelance character design, if a client selects your work, you won't have enough time to redo things in 3D."

TIPS - If you Drawing creatures in human form makes them recognizable due to the scientific principle that humans naturally relate to human-like shapes.

53

# DRAW FROM REFERENCE

To draw human figures from reference, start with basic shapes, establish proportions, outline a skeleton, add volume, refine details, and incorporate shading. Practice regularly to improve anatomy and accuracy in designs.

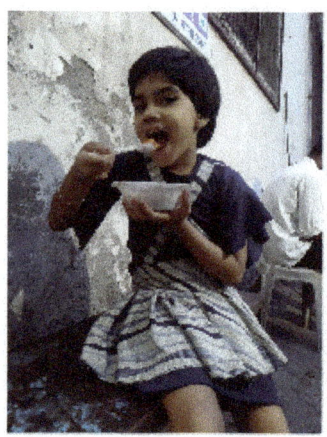

**Draw-Draw & Sketch-Sketch**
As a student, practice consistently by drawing and sketching regularly. It enhances skills, builds confidence , and improves artistic growth.

**TIPS**
When you draw rough, you start to see things more clearly.

# PERSPECTIVE FOR CHARACTER

To draw characters in perspective, start by creating box shapes to help measure where the character will be placed. Then, set the horizon line and vanishing points,

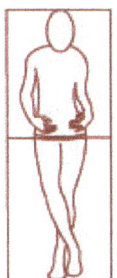 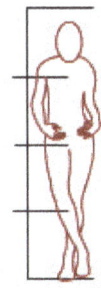 

Divide the character into parts to build and understand structure.

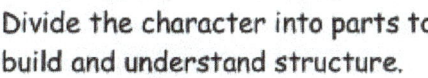

Drawing roughly helps you visualize and understand shapes and proportions.

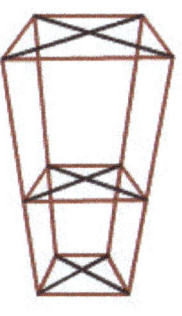

Adjust the proportions, and focus on depth to make the character look 3D.

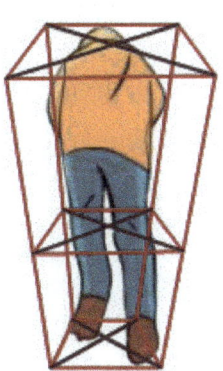

Character doesn't go outside the grid lines and follows the outer lines for proper placement and proportion.

 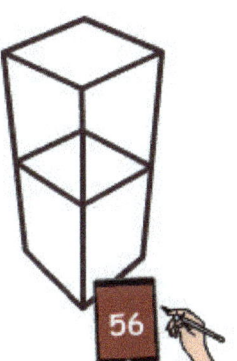

56

## PERSPECTIVE FOR CHARACTER

The box grid method helps you break down complex forms (like a human body or other characters) into simpler geometric shapes (primarily boxes or cubes) to maintain proportionality and perspective regardless of the viewing angle.

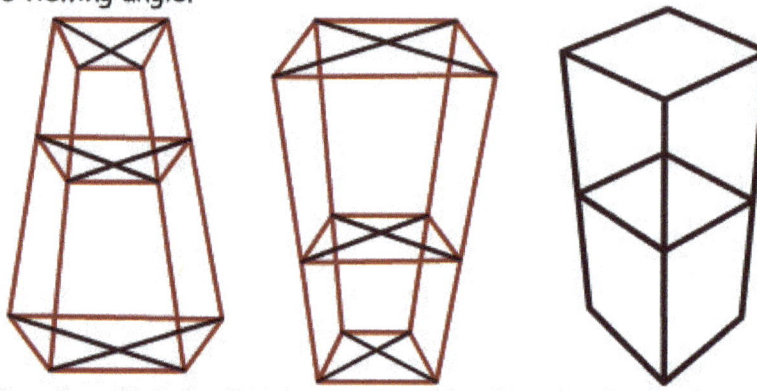

The Key steps include defining perspective, forming basic shapes, refining anatomy, and adding details. Important factors are maintaining volume, gesture, anatomical accuracy, and managing perspective distortion to create dynamic, believable character designs.

## PLACEING CHARACTER IN PRESPECTIVE

Perspective walking toward the camera is mostly used in animation but can also be applied in creating perspective cartoon designs. It creates depth by adjusting the character's movement, making them appear larger and closer to the viewer.

Adjust the character's size according to these lines.

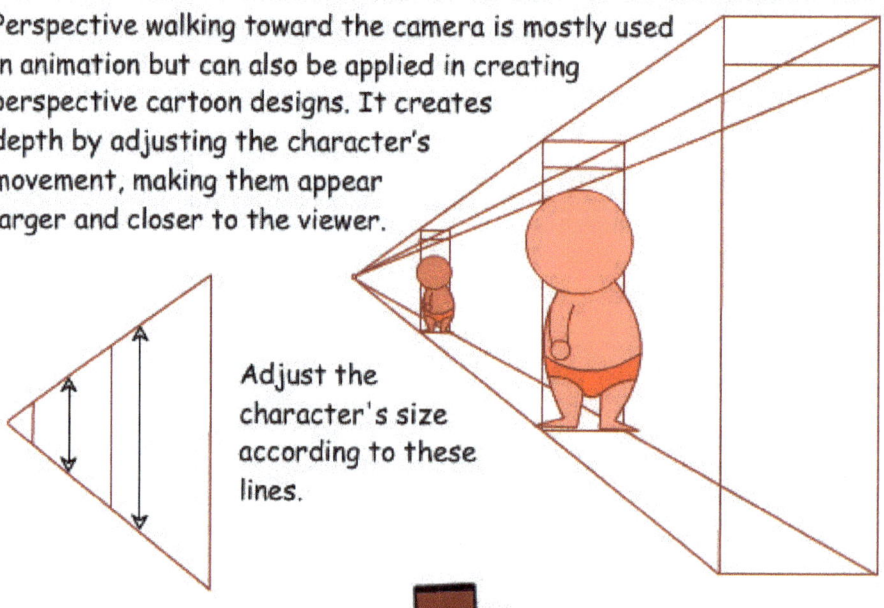

## Cute Character

### Exaggerated Feature

**PHOTO CHARACTER**

When creating Exaggerating features enhances their personality. For cute characters, a larger cranium compared to the mouth evokes innocence, while villains or "badasses" may have more intense, sharper features. Distorted traits like oversized eyes, heads, and limbs emphasize emotions and humor, making characters dynamic and expressive.

A disproportionately large head compared to the body often suggests innocence, wisdom, or comedic effect and Oversized Eyes are often drawn larger than usual to convey emotions like surprise, shock, or excitement.

Characters may be drawn with extreme poses, like a stretched body or slumped shoulders, to convey personality or energy.

## UNIQUE TRAITS

If you design several character together make sure the overall approach
To make your character stand out in a crowd, focus on distinctive elements
like silhouette, color palette, facial expression, unique accessories,
posture, height, and hairstyle. These traits, such as a different stance,

Vibrant colors, or unique details, help your character maintain
individuality while blending into the group.

## APPEAL

Appeal is most important aspect when we are making eyes mouth and
mouth and nose of the character look at this two drawings

Balance the overall geometry         The space between the eyes doesn't
by adjusting the leg spacing.         make the character appear natural.

Eyes reflect emotions.                Asymmetrical eyes.

## Draw Non-Living Things

## SMOKE

Smoke follows a variety of patterns, moving upward and gently dissipating cartoon smoke, use soft, curving lines that flow in a specific direction.

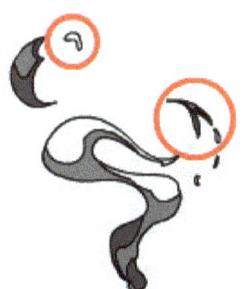
Overlapping Twist

Curving Lines

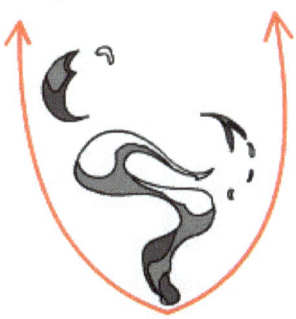
Move Foward

Creating overlapping and twisting sections for a dynamic look. Divide the smoke into disconnected parts for a fluffy texture. Add exaggerated squiggly lines or spirals for a whimsical, playful effect.

## WATER

In cartoons, use wavy lines, arcs, and splashes. Incorporate fluidity with zig-zag lines for movement. For splashes, draw small, curved, irregular lines shooting outward from an impact point, with droplets flying off to emphasize dynamic, playful water effects.

Wavy Lines

Zig-Zag movement

Water drops

The breakup of the water should be uneven; the water is displaced from the center outwards, and as the stone sinks, the mud travels downward.

Irregular shapes

Flying off

# FIRE

Start with sharp, pointed tips and curving teardrop shapes, varying in size and overlapping. To create movement, use flowing, upward-curving lines that get thinner as they rise, giving the flames a dynamic, energetic appearance. This adds a sense of motion and intensity to the fire.

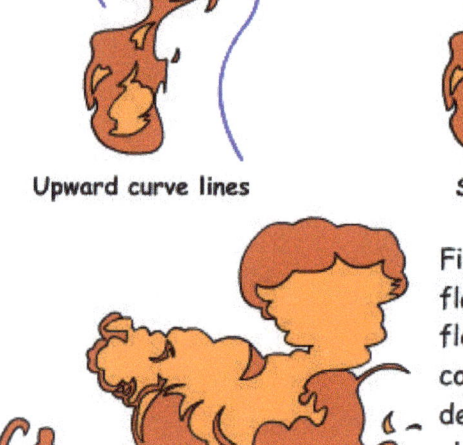

Upward curve lines    Sharp    Energetic Appearance

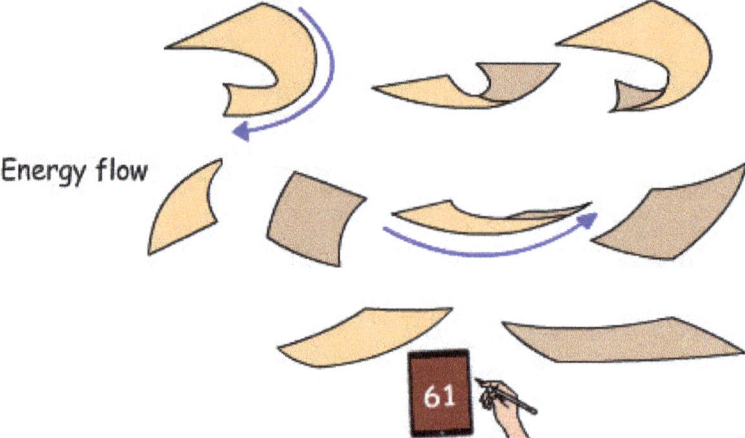

Fire, start with teardrop-shaped flames and add curves to make them flow upward. Layer flames, using bright colors like yellow, orange, and red. Add details such as smoke, sparks, and glowing effects.

# PAPER

Paper or a leaf encounters a lot of air resistance due to their light weight, which affects their movement. A paper cannot fall in a straight line when it hits the ground.

Energy flow

61

# LEAF

To Create a leaf at any angle, start with the basic shape and central vein. Adjust the outline to reflect the angle and add curves along the edges to represent the fold or curl.

Curves lines

Opposite Curves

In a side view, show the leaf's width and top curvature, with horizontal or diagonal veins. In a top view, display the tip and width, with veins extending outward. For a bent leaf, use a curved central vein.

## BREAKDOWN REAL LIFE THINGS INTO DRAWINGS

If human beings are not familiar with the subject matter, then we can easily play with the object or subject. People see animals like cats and dogs every day, but they are not familiar with creatures of other kinds. Eg, dinosaurs.

Real-life objects into drawings involves simplifying complex forms into basic shapes, focusing on key details, and understanding the proportions and structure.

### FOUR STEPS TO DRAW REAL LIFE THINGS

Step - 1) Observe the Object Carefully

Step - 2) Simplify the Structure

Step - 3) Measure proportions & Angles

Step - 4) Exaggerate the object

# CARTOON CAR CONVERSION

Cartooning a car involves simplifying and exaggerating its features to create a more playful and expressive look focus on stylizing key features, adding vibrant colors, and creating a fun, whimsical look.

Start with Basic car shape for the body of the car.

Later add two circles for the wheels

Simplify the car by drawing oval windows and a curved windshield. Exaggerate details like large, round headlights and a smiling grille. Refine with bold, smooth lines, adding features like exhaust pipes or antennae.

## CARTOON BIKE CONVERSION

Start by drawing large circles for the wheels, and lines for the handlebars and pedals. Exaggerate the features by making the wheels larger.

The handlebars more curved. Add quirky details like exaggerated pedals and a cute face on the wheel.

## Silhouettes

If you don't have an idea for a character, start with silhouettes basically black drawings. Silhouettes are a great way to generate ideas. Design is a language.

Sometimes, it's important to add design features that capture your audience's attention and make them think. Silhouettes help define perspective. Always keep in mind what you're aiming to achieve. If something doesn't fit your character, change it.

Silhouettes assist in experimenting with various layouts and structures, while also setting the emotional tone of a design. They can evoke feelings of intrigue, tension, or simplicity. Try to make many Silhouettes of same design keywords.

## ADVANTAGES OF SILHOUETTES

If the silhouette is strong, then sometimes the details are not as important as the image itself. Silhouettes make it easy for your audience to instantly recognize the good guy and the bad guy. Therefore, silhouettes must be very, very strong.

Keep silhouettes in mind when drawing. Understand how the human eye functions— It first focuses on silhouettes.

The human brain processes silhouettes quickly. People can easily identify figures or objects based on their outline, helping to communicate ideas faster.

Silhouettes create contrast between a dark figure and a light background can make the subject stand out and capture attention.

Silhouettes remove unnecessary details, focusing purely on the shape and form of a subject

# CONSTRUCTION OF SILHOUETTES

Designers should master presenting silhouettes, combining shapes and forms to craft impactful, engaging visuals for the audience.

Primary Silhouettes

Secondary Silhouettes

Tertiary Silhouettes

These are not contributing factors to the silhouettes; they help construct the silhouettes.

These are the secondary silhouettes, which break the forms. Secondary details quickly help you achieve your selling points.

Third-level details are found within the second level and contribute to adding the final touches, enhancing the overall finish of the design.

Note
your brain takes microseconds to figure things out.

This is how details progress

Secondary and tertiary knowledge is derived from cultural references Silhouettes and secondary details define functions.

As an audience, when you are looking for something specific, you are culturally programmed to understand strong visual language. You identify things with the help of prominent secondary details.

Remember, you click on things that grab your attention. This happens in a fraction of a second. Visual focus leads the eye, allowing us to control where the viewer looks.

constructing a silhouette is about simplifying a subject down to its most basic, recognizable form while ensuring it communicates its identity, emotion, and function effectively. It's a balance of abstraction and clarity.

## Keep things simple, and add complexity later.

Modifying the rocket's size, whether enlarging or reducing it, can throw off the design's balance. It impacts proportions, making it harder to maintain harmony and control, which may result in a less unified outcome.

Keep the design simple by avoiding excessive detail. The computer serves as the key element that maintains balance within the overall composition, ensuring the design remains clear, focused, and visually harmonious.

Balance proportion is Important

## Challanges

No-undo challenges are a great exercise. The first 5 to 10 minutes can be horrifying, especially if you're a beginner, but you have to believe in yourself and your skills. This will take your abilities to the next level.

NOTE: If you're only working on one drawing at a time, you can get stuck in it and become too absorbed. If something goes wrong with that piece or with your client, it can put you in a bad mood, and you may no longer enjoy the process. This is especially dangerous for those who are in the learning stage.

## TIPS

1. Set Time Limits: Set a fixed amount of time for each drawing. This prevents you from becoming too attached to one piece and promotes a more laid-back, balanced approach to the creative process.

2. Create Multiple Pieces at Once: Work on several drawings at once. this flexibility your focus and allows you to shift your attention if you encounter difficulties with one piece.

3. Seek Feedback Early: Share your work with peers, mentors, or clients during the creation process instead of waiting until it's completed. This can offer valuable perspectives and lessen the emotional attachment to the final piece.

4. Accept Imperfection: Remind yourself that not every piece has to be flawless or live up to high standards. Embracing mistakes can create a more enjoyable and relaxed creative atmosphere.

# C - 2  The Art of Expressions

### Expressions

Disney animators can draw poses and expressions very well because they are skilled at capturing both photographic and realistic poses. They have a lot of experience and understand how the human body works, allowing them to create expressions that look lifelike. Human faces are easily recognizable because we are familiar with the subject matter.

**EVERY ILLUSTRATOR AND ARTIST DEALS WITH EXPRESSIONS**

### Emotions sheets

Any emotion is the hardest to draw because human beings are familiar with human emotions. Emotions bring your drawing to life and create an experience for your viewer, making them feel happy, sad, etc. Through these emotions, the viewer can easily read your character.
first establishing the structure of the face before adding facial expressions. Many artists, especially beginners, make the mistake of jumping straight to expressions. The correct approach is to first define the basic geometric shapes of the head and ears, as these help position facial features properly. The face should be viewed as a three-dimensional form, with features sculpted on top of the basic head structure. This approach ensures the face looks realistic and balanced, allowing for more accurate and proportionate expressions.

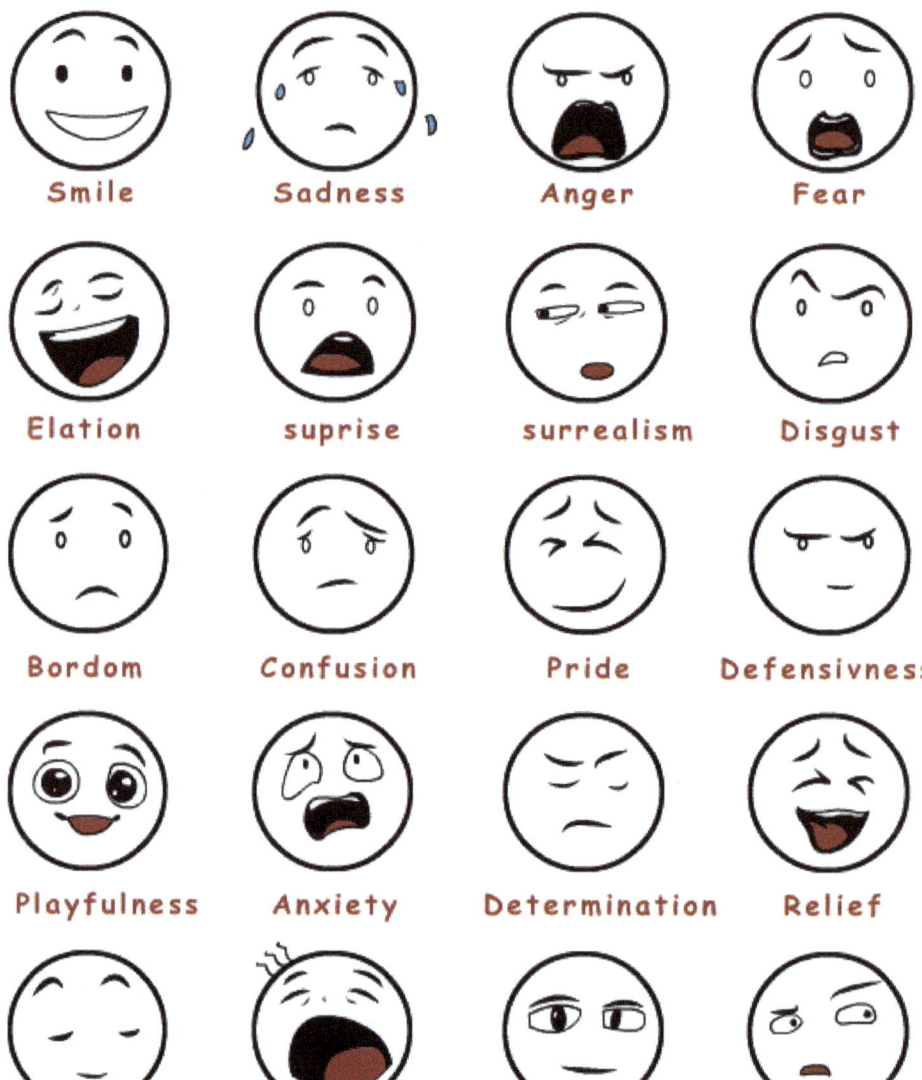

Excitement

embarrassment

Nostalgia

Skepticism

Curiosity

Hopefulness

Reluctance

Admirations

Overwhelm

## line of action

The Line of action is an imaginary line that is placed on a body or a figure to indicate the direction of energy movement or the orientation of a pose.

It guides the viewer's eye creates a more dynamic, fluid representation, and captures the essence of movement and energy in a figure

The line of action may extend from an upper torso in a circular motion this enables them to demonstrate the movement of the body.

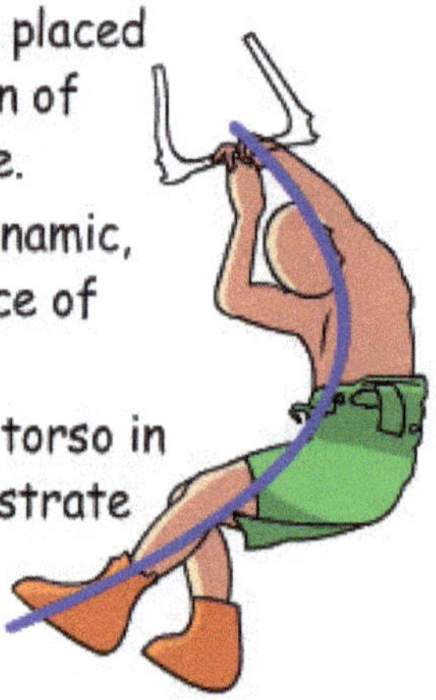

## Body Language

Body language is a form of communication that is expressed without the use of words it is characterized through an individual's bodily posture, movements, gestures, facial expression as well as physical actions. In relation to character design, body language is critical in the plot since it shows how a character is built and aids in the performance in which the character feels during the interaction. In this way, a character can be presented in a more lively, credible, and engaging way to the viewer.

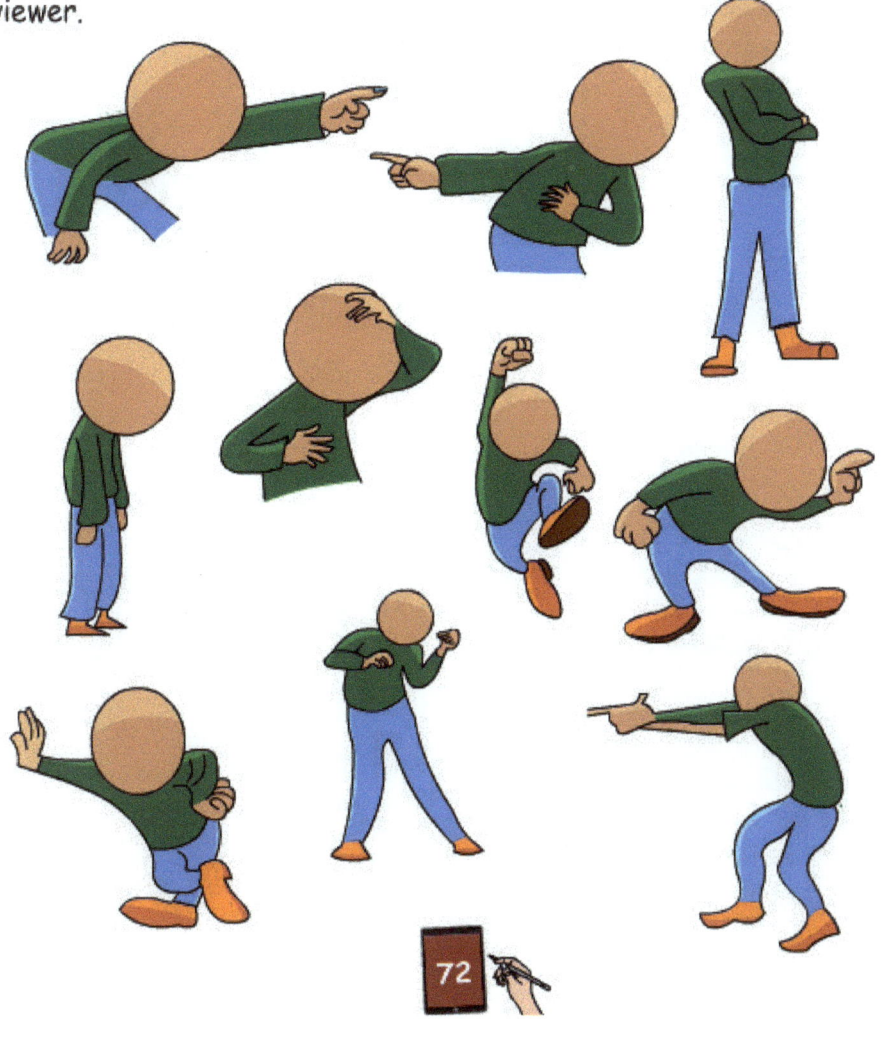

# Emotional Tone

Emotional Tone conveyed through a work of art, design, or storytelling It reflects the feelings or emotions evoked in the audience by the characters.

Add emotion based on character shapes or facial outlines.

Equal eyes, mouth for normal.

Character shapes must match the emotions.

Add emotion based on character shapes or facial outlines.

Exaggerated features emphasizing humor or emotion.

When you draw emotions, make sure the eyes and mouth are constructed in similar sizes.

When exaggerating a character, enlarge the mouth or eyes, or make them different.

## Keyword for design

Beginner artists don't plan enough without design keywords, which can lead to wasting a lot of time. Many times, artists burn out with no results due to a lack of strong art direction, resulting in a scattered art department. Remember, experimenting with design without a clear direction wastes both money and time.

First, identify who your audience is.
(1) Cultural
(2) Exaggeration
(3) Flashy
(4) Functional
(5) Human stories
(6) higher details
(7) Mature
(8) Wild Rider
(9) Slower Race
(10) Pure fun
(11) Younger

Now, Writing things on a paper before started is help a lot Set your time and improve remember your 1,000th drawing is better than your first drawing, guaranteed.

When you're struggling with a design, it's helpful to tackle the easier parts first. This approach boosts morale and keeps your confidence high , preventing frustration. By stepping back and evaluating what's working, you can gain clarity and motivation to keep moving forward. Personally, when I draw, I feel happy and use it as an opportunity to train and improve. During the initial stages of creating, remember that only you see the work—there's no need to worry about outside opinions. Focus on personal progress and growth, as early mistakes are part of the learning process and will lead to improvement over time.

Keywords help designers concentrate on important aspects of their work , guiding decisions like style and features. They also ensure consistency across various design stages, keeping elements aligned throughout the project.

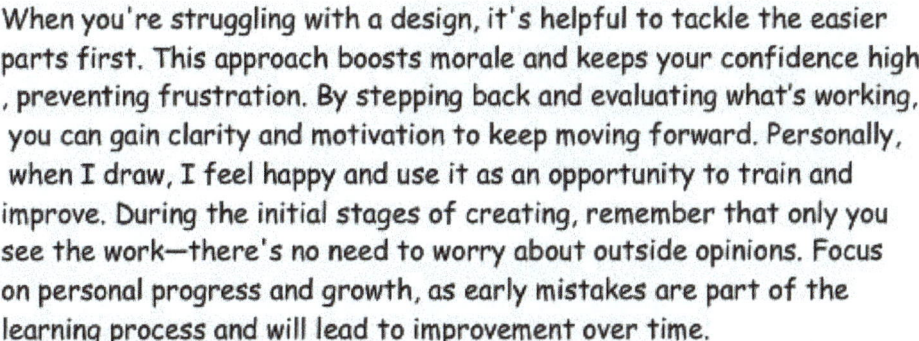

# Keyword for design

keywords serve as powerful tools that guide the creative process,

enhance communication and writing keywords help to keep artist on track and focus only on the important words and design things around it.

(1) Astronaut - Human exploration and adventure in space.
(2) Celestial Bodies - Stars, moons, and planets, providing a rich tapestry of shapes and colors to explore.
(3) Space Colony - Human habitats in space, exploring futuristic architecture and community design.
(4) Stargate - A portal for traveling between worlds, evoking themes of adventure and exploration.
(5) Gravity - The force that pulls objects together, influencing movement and structure in art.
(6) Stealth Ship - A spacecraft designed for covert operations, with a dark, angular design and advanced cloaking technology.

Similarly,

(1) Conflict
(2) Artificial Intelligence
(3) Upgrade Modules
(4) Reprogramming
(5) Factory chamber
(6) Discussion

(1) Exploration
(2) Asteroid Field
(3) Spacecraft
(4) Modular Design
(5) Interstellar Travel
(6) Robo

## Intellectual Property (IP)

Intellectual Property (IP) refers to creations of the mind, such as inventions, literary and artistic works, designs, symbols, names, and images used in commerce. IP is protected by law through patents, copyrights, trademarks, and trade secrets, allowing creators to control the use of their creations and benefit from them financially.

For Example, The main character from the "God of War" video game series. Kratos is known for his bald head, distinctive tattoos (including a red tattoo that resembles a barcode), and his violent quest for revenge against the gods of Olympus and other mythological figures. The series is famous for its intense combat, rich storytelling, and exploration of themes such as vengeance, redemption, and the consequences of one's actions.

## IP Creation Checklist

(1) WHO IS YOUR AUDIANCE  _____
(2) WHAT IS YOUR BUDGET AND DEADLINE _____
(3) WHAT THE ONE LINE SUMARRY  _____
(4) STORY CONTRAST  _____
(5) TIME PEROID  _____
(6) LIGHTING CONTRAST  _____
(7) CHARACTER CONTRAST  _____
(8) WHAT IS THE HOOK  _____

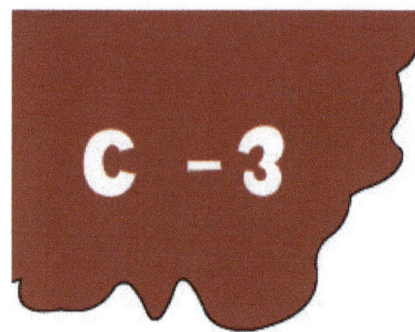

# C-3 Visual Design Fundementals

## Fundementals

Visual Design means creating appealing and effective designs using various principals & rules. Visuals communicate message and evoke emotions.

Pro Artist just takes 2 min to fix your mistakes but this 2 min carry 20 years of experience.

Mastering the fundamentals of visual design may seem tedious and It takes a lot of time to master But the efforts pays off in the long run. Fundamentals serve as the foundation for all design work. Understanding concepts like prespective, form, horizontals markers & much more are building block of every design.

A strong foundation allows you to push boundaries while maintaining clarity in your work and It helps you convey messages communicates ideas clearly and effectively and emotions through visual elements Understanding fundamental principles equips you with the tools to find creative solutions in various contexts.

Bad prespective

Good prespective

Thinks about how you show up the things. there are some artists who can simply point, and their paintings look like photorealism because they know how the fundamentals work.

## Prespective

Prespective create the illusion of depth and space on a flat surface without prespective it is harder to do things correctly.

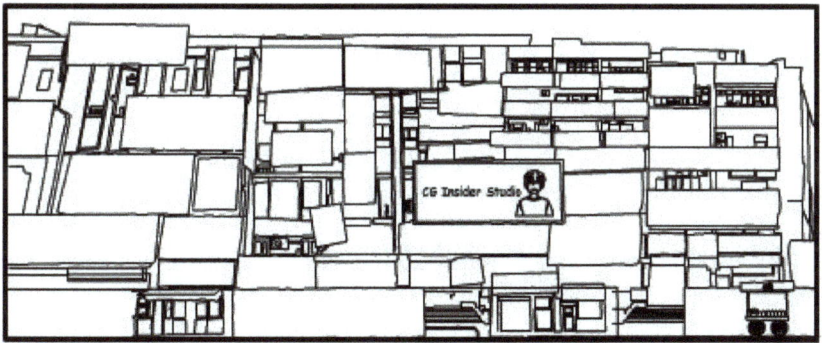

Perspective is like your eyeball, the better you draw, so viewer eyes can understand well. good prespective make things believable, Prespective is all about starting with nothing and coming-up with somthing amazing.

## One-Point Prespective

All the parallel lines in the composition converge toward a single point on the horizon, known as the vanishing point. It helps create the appearance of space and makes the drawing appear more realistic.

Tip :- When dealing with prespective start with very standard warmup design.

## KEY ELEMENTS OF ONE-POINT PERSPECTIVE

1. Horizon Line: This is the eye level of the viewer and represents where the sky meets the ground. It runs horizontally across the picture plane.

Horizon Line

All lines converge at a single vanishing point. Perspective gives 2D drawingsa 3D appearance.

2. **Vanishing Point:** The single point on the horizon line where parallel lines appear to converge. In one-point perspective, all lines that are parallel to the viewer's line of sight will lead to this point.

# BUILD ONE-POINT PRESPECTIVE

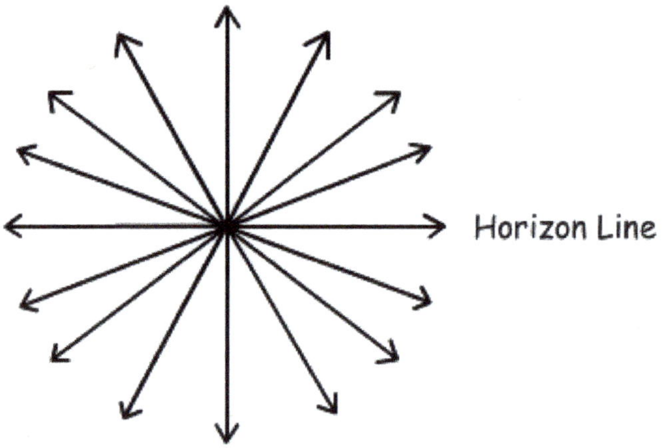

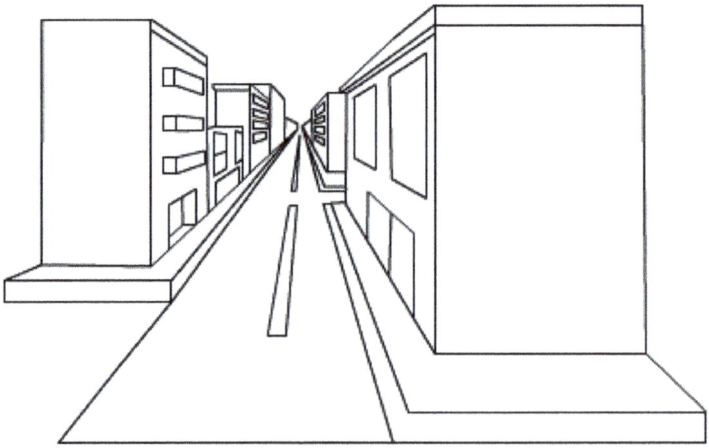

# Two-Point Prespective

The most commonly used prespective system. it is used to rotating the things. Two vanishing points are used, typically located on the horizon line. These two points are where the parallel lines of the object recede into the distance.

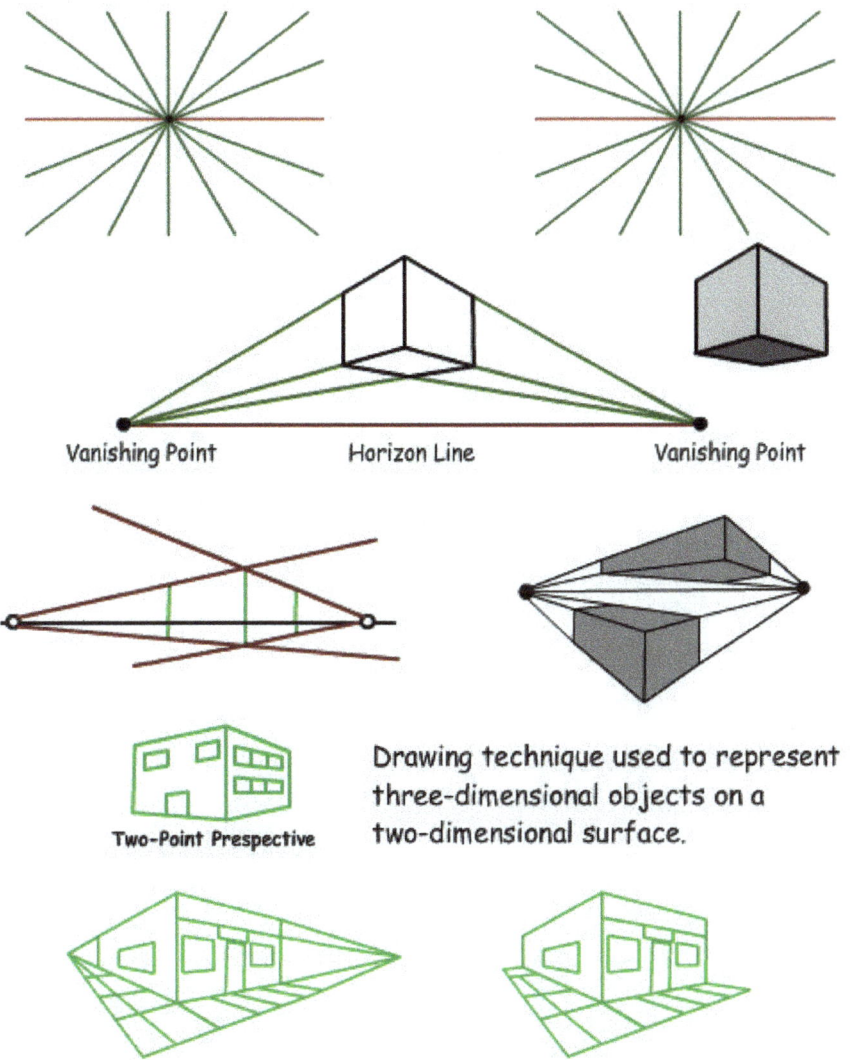

Drawing technique used to represent three-dimensional objects on a two-dimensional surface.

Tip :- When dealing with prespective start with very standard warmup design.

# Three-Point Prespective

All of this helps us describe where things are placed. Three-point perspective adds another vanishing point, which is in the sky or floor This is good for representing something that is upward or downward.

Three-point perspective uses three vanishing points. It is used for extreme angles. Two vanishing points are placed on the horizontal line, and the third vanishing point is located either above or below the horizon line. This creates a more dynamic and dramatic effect.

Three-dimensional space, we refer to axes as the reference lines used to define the position of points or object.

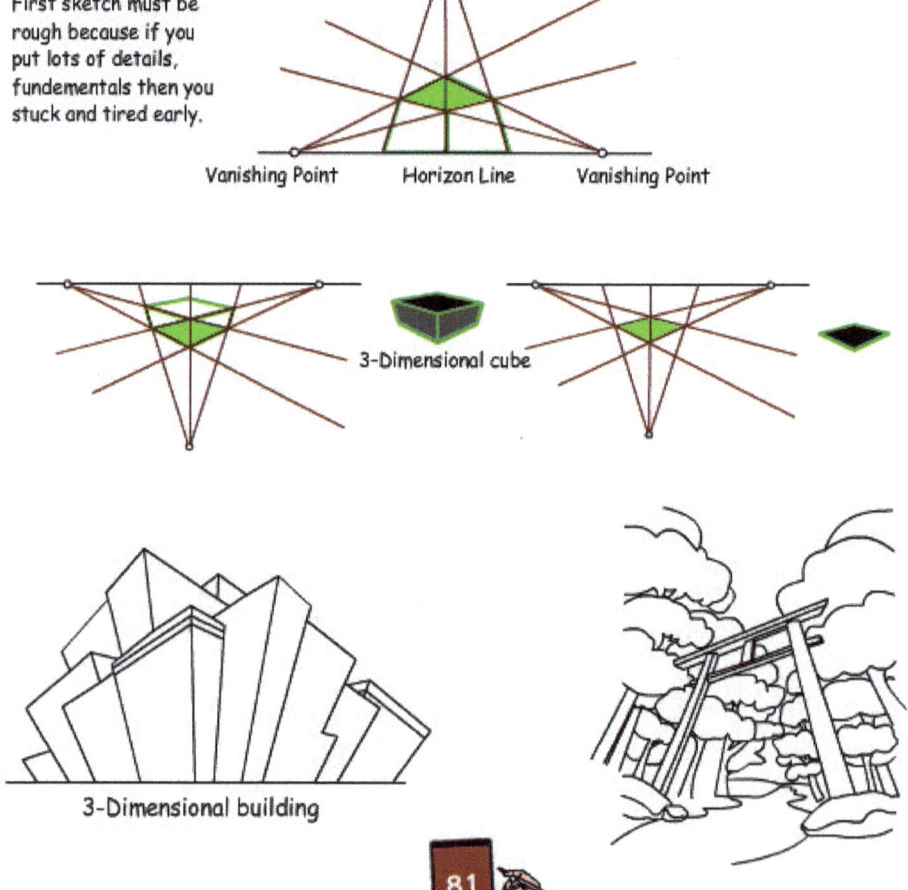

Note
First sketch must be rough because if you put lots of details, fundementals then you stuck and tired early.

## Horizontals

Horizontals line are straight lines. This are typically used to represent stability. simply and easy mistakes is not knowing about Horizons. Horizontals lines make compositions more dynamics

Mobile photography

Horizontals line

It is your eye level. just know about Horizontals. identify which work best for your scenes.

This princpal is applicable for all kind of things wether it is photograph 2D illistration or even in 3d game trailer.

Mobile photography    2d Animation    3d Animation

This are three different drawing of Horizontals.

Self-learning artists mentally visualize vanishing points and horizontal lines to understand perspective, guiding composition and creating depth in their work.

Tip - Don't start with white canvas they are too bright, instead have some paper material this will give values.

Many beginners artists neglect fundamentals, leading to common mistakes in their work, resulting in a lack of depth and realism. such as distorted proportions or flat compositions, which can make their work appear unrealistic or lacking in depth. Mastering these fundamentals is crucial for creating believable art. First, identify the horizontal lines, and then make sure the perspective is up to mark.

## COMMON MISTAKES IN HORIZONTALS

Not having vanishing points in your scene means that the perspective is not defined, which can make the scene appear flat and lacking depth. Vanishing points help create the illusion and depth by guiding.

Have multiple Horizontals lines.

Lack of perspective.

Tips - Most of the time the photographers is standin the head level or below.

## Markers

Markers can be used to guide design and used to grab attention, emphasize key aspects, or provide clarity.

Markers help you to build confidence by creating a bit of chaos on the page before you start. it is mental exercise.

Markers allows you to thinks out loud on paper, but without committing 100% to the design. Marker are X- Rays of prespectice ,Markers put couple of prespective guild lines in the canvas.

Markers

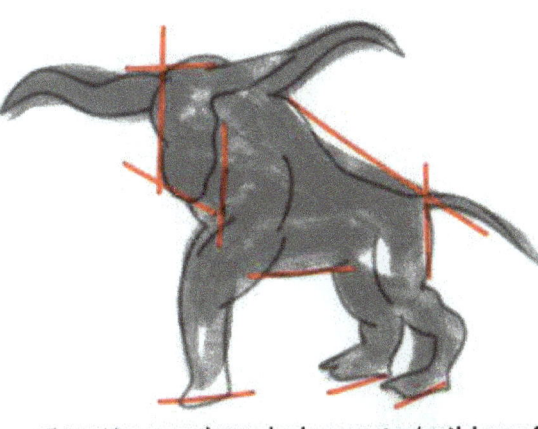

Creating art or design can be challenging. It requires skill, and patience, to practice to master the techniques of drawing, sketching, and designing. The "Marker" can be a starting point for creating a design, which is often a difficult step.

Creating markers help you to build confidence by creating a bit of chaos on the page. before you start it is more like mental exercise. First create couple of silloutes and then we apply markers on that this keep things in flow.

Allow your line drawings to be loose, giving yourself the freedom to experiment, explore new ideas, and embrace creativity. Markers are one technique, but there are many others in the vast design universe.

# CHARACTERSTIC OF MARKERS

Marker build siloutes very faster then sketchs - Markers quickly create bold silhouettes, allowing for faster visualization and design development compared to more detailed, time-consuming sketches.

Markers help you think in volume, not just outlines. - Markers encourage thinking in terms of volume and form, helping to visualize three-dimensional space rather than focusing solely on outlines.

It is must easier to build strong silloutes using markers. If you get better with this approach you can try many things. once you practice this techniques then change or apply variations.

Marker help us to gent concentrations - Markers help us focus by providing bold, clear lines that guide attention, enhancing concentration during the creative design process.

TIP: If you're stuck on a design, work on the easier sections first.

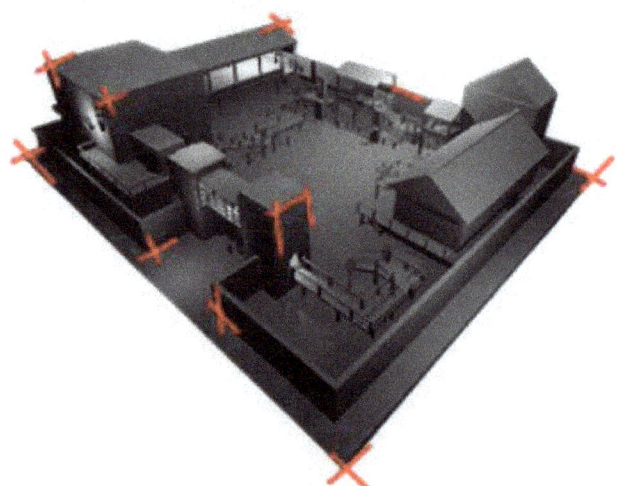

Initial marker strokes may not appear in the final design, but they are crucial for shaping the creative process.

## Selling points

Selling points is what your viewer is want to see first. Selling point define first then later define background. use high and low contrast values to make viewer to look at the things.

Selling point define first then later define background. use high and low contrast values to make viewer to look at the things.

Human eyes work in patterns, and when you make things readable for your audience, things become more interesting. Make sure the value is clearly defined. We will discuss this in more detail in Chapter 4.

## STRATEGY

Working with No patterns

Working with patterns

Audience might get confused about where to look.

Design a clear vision for the audience.

Try to figure out your own composition and entertain your audience through your design.

If you want your viewer to look at your focal points then lead the viewer eyes.

A brighter focal point in a selling point refers to the key element in a design that stands out and captures the viewer's attention.

Focal point = Brighter

A darker focal point in design uses muted or low-contrast elements to subtly guide attention. It creates depth, mystery, and emphasizes secondary features, balancing the composition without being too bold.

Ground elements = Darker

Identify which character or object takes up the most space on your canvas, as this will make it easier to balance the other elements. The end result is not just an object it is communication.

Selling point elements are balanced.

A selling point must be carefully defined in every design, as it guides the viewer's eye to the key subject matter. It serves as the central element that tells a story, consistently communicating the core message or feature across the design.

The first sketch should be rough because focusing too much on details and fundamentals too early can lead to creative block Starting with a loose concept allows flexibility to refine the selling point later without getting overwhelmed. selling point provide a clear sense of the story and a concise message, ensuring the audience quickly understands.

Composition imbalanced

The Castle placement in the corner creates an imbalanced layout, and adding supporting elements may distract the viewer. Using every space carefully is essential to maintain balance and focus in the composition.

Composition imbalanced

The larger character size suggests the camera is closer, creating a sense of personal connection towards the character or emphasis on the character.

Composition balanced

The small character size gives the impression that the camera is placed far from the character, creating distance.

## Form & Grids

## FORM

Forms means the shapes and structures of objects or element that define the visual and physical characteristics of a design which can be three-dimensional or two-dimensional.

While drawing a complex creature make sure arrange them in forms of lines. this will helps to understand forms. Human eyes follow forms, as a designer you have to follow some kind of design aspect because human beings understand forms easily.

Concepts art usually consists of 3d forms this make things look more belivable.

| Ideal forms | First |
|---|---|
| Fundementals | Second |

Just capure the over all things

### DRAWING DETAILS IS NOT THE HARDER PART. DRAWING FORMS IS THE HARDER PART.

When it comes to design, it's always about forms and energy flow. Keep fluidity in your drawing to maintain harmony and balance. When dealing with forms, things may get messy, and that's okay. Sometimes everything gets messed up, and many students give up at this point, but you have to push through and let your masterpiece emerge.

Remember - One of the most important parts of design is the forms.

In design, forms come first as the foundation. Once the basic forms are established, you can apply design fundamentals like balance, contrast, and alignment to refine and strengthen the composition.

### EXERCISE -

At the beginning stage, do 100+ drawings of tree roots to better learn forms.

# GRIDS

Grids are used to organize and align elements within the artwork. grids act as a guideline for artists, making the design process more efficient

Prepare perspective grids in advance to save time when working digitally. this is especially useful when working digitally.

If you want your rough drawing to look good, match it with 3D by using perspective grids. If you understand composition fundamentals, your work will directly align with 3D. When you draw in 2D with grids and later use it in 3D, the shot will almost look the same.

A grid helps ensure consistency, proportion, and balance across characters, backgrounds, and scenes.

Some students follow pro artist techniques without understanding them, skipping important steps and picking up bad habits.

# REPETATIVE FORMS

Repetitive forms work well in certain design languages. These forms, which humans naturally find comforting to the eyes, are often used in sci-fi animation movies. They create a flow that ensures the mind and eyes don't get confused.

In cartoons, making things look realistic is not as fun.

Forms help us identify and tell a story easily. Create forms that serve a function by first identifying the energy flow. Repeating forms guide the viewer's eye smoothly through the composition, creating a pleasing flow Repeating certain shapes in characters, like round heads or uniform body proportions, helps make the design recognizable

## Establishing Shots

Establishing shots means rithum of the scene establishing shots are essential tools in visual storytelling that guide the audience to understanding the space and mood before the main action happens.

some time you have to design r or more different story with same type of mood or feeling for video game or for animated short flims.

### THINGS KEEP IN MIND WHILE DESIGNING ESTABLISHING SHOTS

1.) Clarity of situation - The primary purpose of an establishing shot is to clearly communicate the setting or situation to the audience.

2.) Camera - What kind of camera are we dealing with?

3.) Composition: A well-composed shot directs the viewer's attention to the important details

*Have some goals before stablishing a shots!*

When you are designing, put yourself in the right mindset. The first few hours of design are critical in establishing the rest of the project.

It's all about trying things and figuring out what works best for you and what doesn't! Combine a lot of experience and see which works best.

### THINGS TO AVOID WHILE MAKING ESTABLISHING SHOTS

1.) Distracting Elements: Avoid unnecessary details that draw attention away from the central focus of the shot.

2.) Avoid Overcomplication: Keep the shot simple.

3.) Confusing Composition: A cluttered or poorly framed shot can leave the audience

4.) Inconsistent Style: Establishing shots should align with the mood and visual style of the rest of the production.

5.) Mixing two shot: The purpose is to set the scene quickly and clearly, so overly intricate camera movements,

REMEMBER - After a certain amount of time your style is born.

## SHOT DESIGN

Start with small things and later extend the things. In cartoon creation, various shots help convey emotion and action. Wide shots set the scene, medium shots focus on character interaction, and close-ups highlight emotions or details. An Extreme Close-Up emphasizes small details to heighten emotion or importance, while a Master Shot captures the entire scene, setting context and providing a foundation for other shots in the sequence.

## ALL KIND OF SHOTS

Wide Shot

Establishing shots

Full shots

medium full shot

Medium Closeup shots

Close up shot

Extreme closeup

Master shot

**Wide shots position** - The subject farther away from the camera to visually represent its relationship with the environment. this is usually used to represent the scale of the subject. this is used to introduce distance and deep.

**Establishing shots** - This is enough to establish the time, geography, and the subject's relationship to the environment. It is very important for the introduction of any scene.

**Full shots** - In which the subject's body is shown from top to bottom, are used to convey the character's body language.

**Medium full shots** - This shot Capture the subject from the top to the waist. It is a neutral shot, typically showing from the chest to the head, and is mostly used in animated film

**SHOT DESIGN**

**Medium closeup shots(MCU)** - This shot reduce distractions and focus on the character's details. they are ideal for capturing reactions and emphasizing emotions or expressions.

**Close up shots** - This shots mostly consist of eye level and are good for representing drama. They focus on small details, such as the face, to intensify emotions and create a personal connection.

**Extreme close up shots** - Extreme close-up shots isolate specific areas, such as the lips, nose, or eyes. They can also focus on objects to emphasize their importance or significance in a scene.

**Master shots** - It is used to establish two things, first the location and second the characters. They confirm the setting of the scene and show how many characters are present.

**Note**
You have to fill every cornor of your Canvas with subjects or ideas

## Camera

Camera placement is a key element in setting up a scene. Placing the camera is a photography lesson, but to create a scene, you need to understand how the camera works. The human eye and the camera both have lenses, and they both work in a same ways. Artists creative freedom to experiment with Camera, enriching the narrative and making the artwork more dynamic and engaging for viewers.

Ultra-wide Lens

### ULTRA-WIDE LENS

- Below 24mm
- Capture wide-prespective which capture lots of informations.

Standard Lens

### STANDARD LENS

- Generally used in photography.
- A 50mm lens on full-frame camera.
- It closly mimics human vision in terms of prespective and depth.

Telephoto Lens

### TELEPHOTO LENS

- Range Between 70mm to 300mm.
- This lens allows to capture Distant subjects with details
- Help to create a unique visuals.

Various lenses offer various effects, such as distorting depth or emphasizing certain elements. This knowledge enhances storytelling by guiding the Audiance attention.

### Point to Remember

- If you don't have control of the camera, crazy things can happen.
- Human eyes work in prespective.

If you lose control of the camera, you can rush your design.

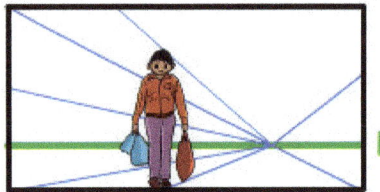
Low Horizon

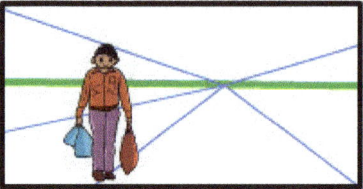
Mid Horizon

> **Remember**
> The horizon line must be in the correct position.

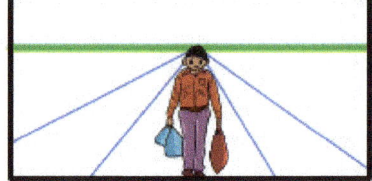
High Horizon

Human eyes work in perspective, so when creating art, the No.1 rule is to check the camera first.

Don't mix two cameras or use two lenses at the same time while creating art on paper or digitally.

Wide- Angle Lens

Standard Lens

Mixing two things we get wired result As good artists, we have to guide the viewer's eyes to the right focus.

Something Wired

If I put the horizon line here and there, it will not be in the right position. The viewer might get confused about where to look.

## REMEMBER
Use all your brain power to figerout the form and different camera angle design required time and Explorations.

## Environment Design

Environment design is creating a space that effectively communicates your message to your audience. it involves creating the visual world that supports the narrative.

First, start with rough sketches to sort out ideas. Once you have the concept, then add the details. Everything goes from top to bottom in the design process.

TIPS

Have real world things and transform it into fun entertment stuff. A lot of entertainment uses history and cultural references—incorporate these into your art. This is how entertainment content is made. Add some demo characters to fill the space.

Example - Mincraft is a largest game if you notice most popular game are built it all on relatable human things.

# DESIGN FORMULA

### Reference + Sketch = Final Product

Environment design formula

References provide inspiration and accuracy, while sketches allow for experimentation and composition and mixing these two things can lead to the creation of the final product

Remember - Ideas must be out use your brain as much as possible in terms of design

When dealing with environment design, your goal must be clear: what do you want to achieve with the environment? Have some color palettes (which we will discuss in more detail in Chapter 4).

When you're drawing on a canvas, organize your elements in a pattern.

Design Follow some pattern

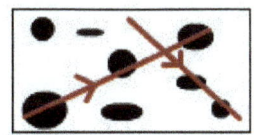
End result distorted Design

If you are working with more than one shot, make sure to maintain a consistent color scheme throughout the environment. Plan your layout to ensure a logical flow that guides the viewer naturally.

Environment design is something that makes you feel something, even without the characters. In design, we can do anything; we can break real-life elements and achieve something interesting by playing with composition, color, shape, and size.

Planning your layout involves arranging elements in a way that directs theaudience attention smoothly, creating a clear, intuitive path that enhances understanding and engagement with the visual content.

Reference

Sketch

Remember – Pros are pros at anything they do that works because they know every rule, having a deep understanding of the rules, which allows them to create back-to-back masterpieces.

Divide the space for different function.

Final Product

Note
The designer's brain is active for only a few hours, and during those few hours, we must decide on the lighting, mood, feeling, and perspective..

We use art as a language to communicate, which is a combination of fundamental knowledge and design Language that leads to great artworks.

## FUNDEMENTAL + DESIGN = MASTERPIECE

Combining a strong fundamentals (foundation) with thoughtful design can lead to exceptional results, whether in art, architecture, product development, or other creative fields.

If you are a beginning artist, the goal is to make every design different from one another, pros have control over things, so as a beginner, you must grab all the skills.

Remember - Creativity doesn't come from a truly tested formula.

If you have a stable design language, then it is easier to create a second design in a short amount of time and produce higher-quality work.

Design idea                                Silhouette

Combining fundamental principles (such as skills, techniques, and knowledge) with thoughtful design (creativity, aesthetics, and functionality) can result in a masterpiece, whether in art, architecture, music, or any other creative field.

When you Mix basic skills, with creative decisions about what to show and how to arrange it, you can make a strong, eye-catching silhouette. This balance of technique and creativity results in a silhouette that is both clear and powerful, making it a great piece of art.

Use design principles like contrast, Balance, Proportion, Rhythm, and Movement emphasis to make the silhouette stand out and create a visually appealing composition. This includes attention to detail, precision,and an understanding of how to use tools effectively. Remember a concept begins with rough ideas, where mistakes are part of the process.

The design formula provides structure to your artistic process and leads to impressive results. Several key concepts can serve as a foundation for creating amazing artwork. Perspective drawing is a technique used by artists and illustrators to create the illusion of depth and space in their designs.

Look at this scene, there is a lot of negative space present. We need to utilize this negative space on the canvas to make scene believable.

Fill the empty space in the design to create a more dynamic scene, but try not to overfill the scene with unwanted elements, as this can distract the audience and make the scene look cluttered, First sketch must be rough because if you put lots of details, fundementals then you stuck and tired early.

# Detail Distributions

Allow the viewer's eye to move naturally from one area to another, guided by the distribution of details.

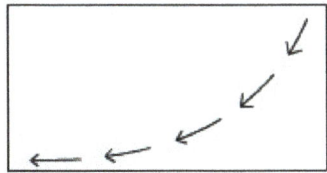 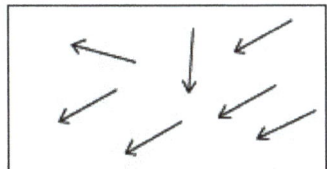

**Single direction energy flow**     **Multi direction energy flow**

Invest your time in improving the selling points, because after the selling points, what matters is the flow of energy. Always remember where your energy is flowing. We can control energy flow with three things:-

- Contrast          - Details          - Lights

This helps differentiate between detailed and less detailed areas. High contrast draws attention, while low contrast recedes into the background.

Add and remove things that create a distracting for human eyes and make sure human eyes are not confused with more details.

Remember - Tiny details makes a huge different in design the last 20% is harder to do than 80%

**Small details can change the overall meaning**

Try to imagine what kind of details you are going to include. In the end, design and creativity are yours. A little logic and minor adjustments will help guide the human eye to read your drawings.

**Drawing with No logic**          **Drawing with logic**

Adding details can be boring because everything you add changes the overall composition very slowly.

Most students spend too much time on unimportant details or elements that don't contribute to the overall message, leading to designs that lack focus, purpose, and ultimately fail to add value.

Create visual cues that help guide the viewer's eye, allowing it to flow naturally across the canvas using leading lines.

Add details to tell a story

Ensure the page is balanced.

Capturing the bigger picture first ensures a strong foundation and overall composition. Once the main structure is set, adding details enhances the design without disrupting its balance or focus.

Remember - Before Adding details make sure you fundementals are correct.

Focusing on the bigger picture, First

There are certain things you shouldn't break; instead, make them in a way that aligns with how the brain and eye work. The closer you are, the clearer the details are. Add more detail only to closer objects becauseif you add too many details, they compete with each other, resulting in no clear perspective or focal point.

When you add details, you always change things around. But if you don't like it, just take it out. It's better than doddling. Adding details means deciding where to place things. Familiarity is important.

Strong shapes provide a foundation, and details enhance the design by supporting its structure and adding visual interest. Adding details including the right elements that support the scene, not random things.

## CONTRAST

Contrast in art means the use of opposite elements that are different like light and dark or big and small to make parts of a picture stand out and grab your attention.

## DETAILS

Distribution detail across the composition or across the artwork. If one area is very detailed, simplify nearby areas to keep the balance and prevent confusing the viewer.

## LIGHTS

Balancing the lights: bright lights can attract attention, while muted low tones can recede, helping to distribute visual weight. adjusting the light and dark areas, you can guide the viewer's focus and create a sense of depth.

## Thumbnil Design

Thumbnail design is a small, preliminary visual representation of a design concept, often used as a quick way to communicate an idea before finalizing the larger design.

When we create entertainment-type pieces where we tell a story clearly, the end result is not artwork, the end result is a product. The thumbnail design is made with high contrast because this makes things readable. It creates a sense of proportion and understanding for the audience. Here's a clearer explanation.

For example, if you add a giant creature, and then add a smaller creature next to it, this will create a sense of scale. In entertainment design, things must be visually clear and understandable to the audience.

Get a cup of coffee, sit in your favorite place, grab your sketchbook and your favorite pen, set a timer of 5 to 10 minutes for your creative process, and brainstorm. Just draw and let the ideas flow.

| FIRST PHASE | SECOND PHASE |
|---|---|
| Rough Phase | Design Phase |

The goal is to finish very detailed line drawings, fitting as many elements as possible. quick sketch it is helpful for visualizing what the final piece will look like.

The rough phase is where initial ideas are quickly sketched out, focusing on concepts, composition, and basic structure. The design phase refines these concepts, adding details, form, perspective, and final touches, resulting in a more polished and cohesive design.

What we design is not a confirmed thing it's an idea. Start with a rough sketch, as it is the most important part of the design process. Once that's done, begin the design, whether it's an environment, creature, or vehicle all follow form, perspective, and definitions.

## WHY IS SOMETHING HAPPENING?

Very early on, when you have a sketch, you must understand what you are showing to the viewers and keep in mind that you have to finish things in a presentable manner.

In Thumbnail design, nothing is original. As a designer, you have to create things that don't bore people. The most important part is that it helps us see things early, like what works and what doesn't.

Many artists focus on producing perfect art, but sometimes imperfect or bad works lead to unexpected results, and creative results. Embracing mistakes can spark new ideas and innovations in the creative process.

Thumbnail free up the stress level, they are part of your creative process. You can see which thumbnails work and which don't. Good students learnthe basic fundamentals and later combine them in design.

## FUNDEMENTAL + DESIGN = MASTERPIECE

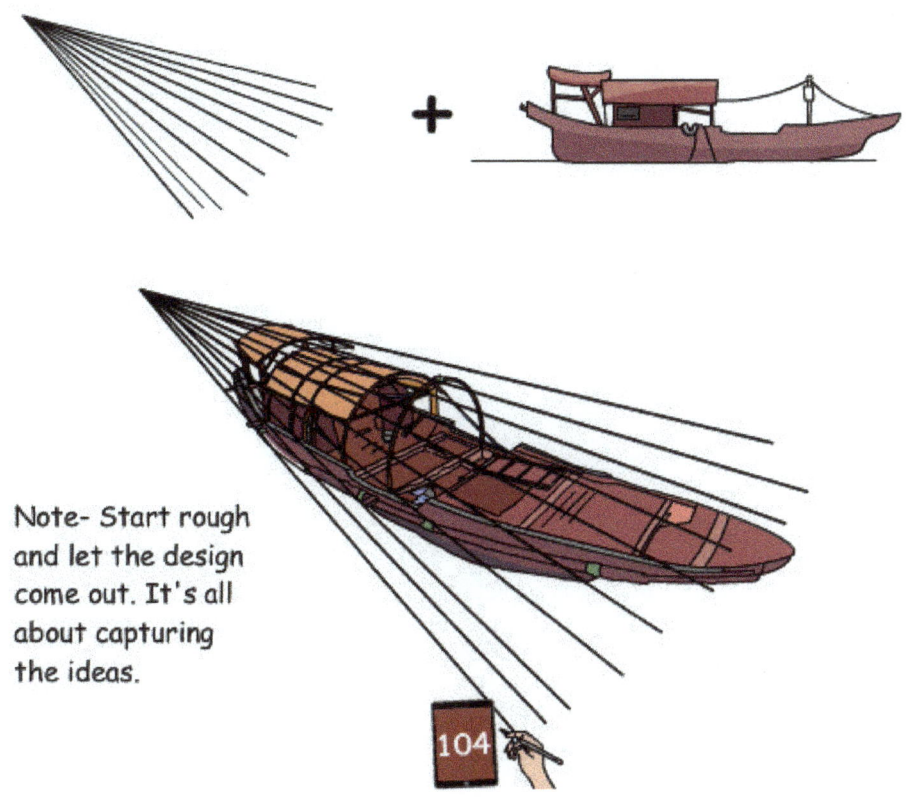

Note- Start rough and let the design come out. It's all about capturing the ideas.

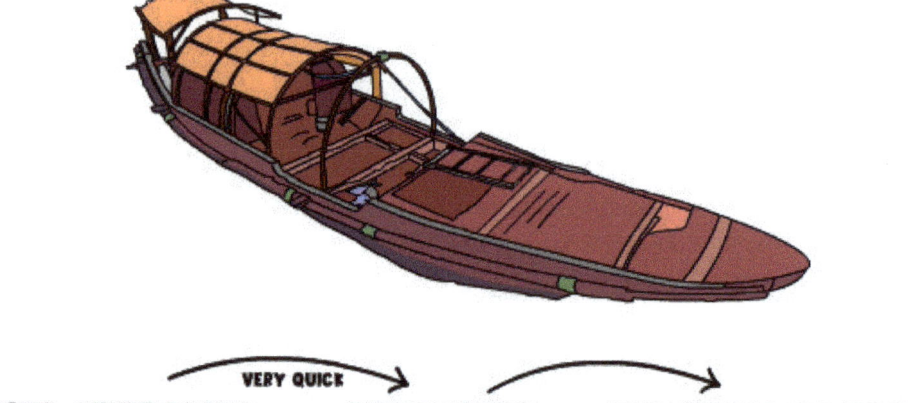

**IDEA GENERATION** → *VERY QUICK* → **THUMBNAILS** → **YOU DO FOR YOURSELF**

Generate thumbnails so your ideas are communicated clearly. Thumbnails allow you to see the idea at an early stage. For thumbnails, nobody cares about the fundamentals or artistic details; the only thing that matters is the idea and design, making it cool and fresh.

Thumbnails work for characters, environments, and everything else. They help generate a lot of ideas in a short amount of time.

We do not render every thumbnail drawing; we only render one, or the one the client likes. The rest of the design is based on your ideas.

**Clients hire us for ideas**

Design as much as you can and see which one the client likes (we discuss this in more detail in Chapter 5).

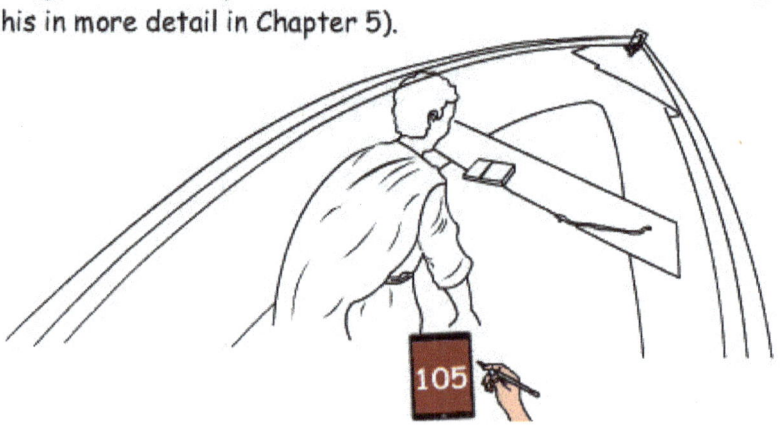

Thumbnail design is not about being different, thumbnail design is about delivering an experience with things that are real and truly exist.

NOTE - Perspective, anatomy, etc. All these things can be fixed in the final stage, which is why we can't focus on them during the thumbnail design process.

Start with a rough thumbnail and an idealization sketch to establish the overall composition. After the rough sketch, the chances of making a mistake are very, very low. Establish a clear vision and design direction, After doing multiple thumbnails, choose one and detail the artwork.

Note: Don't worry about reflections, lighting, or other details, just capture the overall elements.

Kitchen scene idea generation

## Mixing Design

Try to combine two different designs into one artwork. Sometimes cool designs come from mixing things up, so don't worry if things get mixed. Sometimes, mixing environments from multiple countries, such as Japan, America, India, etc., into one design can lead to the creation of a new world. For example, you could have temples from Japan or India in places like America. This kind of approach is mainly used in games, but we can also apply this technique in cartoon creation as well but Mixing the characters is actually complex and is about functionality. At this stage, we have to do a little bit of industrial design.

### PRO ARTISTS USE THE 90/10 RULE TO BALANCE THINGS

**10%**
Unique

**90%**
Relatable to human cultural references or everyday experiences, and grounded design with real-world references.

Take 90% of references from the real world, and 10% from character gestures. (this is where IP comes into play)

### START WITH A WELL ESTABLISHED ICONIC BASE.

90% base Jungle

10% Dinasoure

=

Jurassic park

If you use the vice-versa of the 90/10 principle, then these things are very risky.

# THE 50/50 RULE

Next is the 50/50 formula. At this point, the 90/10 rule is not applicable, which makes these things tough.
Sci-fi movies are made using this formula. It is hard because there are very few references available and kinds of projects are very rare.

 + 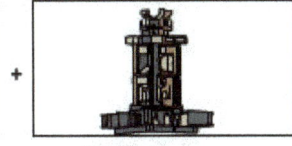 =

50% Si-fi Stuff      50% Future      Sifi movies

TIPS: Consider your portfolio; sci-fi projects are very rare, even if you are a cartoonist or industrial designer.

### SI-FI DESIGN
Designing sci-fi stuff is hard because there are no clear directions and fewer references available.

### FUTURISTIC DESIGN
We don't know much about technological advancement.

### RESULT
Design influences human nature and the evolution of power.

## FIND THE RIGHT BALANCE

Find elements from one time period and combine them with those from another time period. Many games use this to entertain the audience, add some functionality to your design; otherwise, it will look flat.

### MIXING DESIGN FORMULA

**REAL WORLD CULTURE**

Note
In games or cartoon everything is contr-olled by the designer.

Design solution

**TIME PEROID**      **FUNCTION**

This formula will help you create your design language. As a designer, youcannot mix design languages. I repeat, as a designer, you cannot mix designlanguages. Design language is like any other language, such as German or English, which every professional artist develops over time or through a lot of practice.

## Reference

Reference means a source of inspiration, visual material, or example that designers use to guide or inform their work. find historical information from a history book, using it as a reference.

Research and development in design are important because research helps designers understand user needs, while development refines ideas into functional designs. This process leads to better problem-solving, high-quality outcomes.

Use reference images from the internet, but don't copy them, as they are someone else's design.

Organize all your references into majorcategories and gather as many reference as you can, because you never know what kind of project you'll encounter in the future.

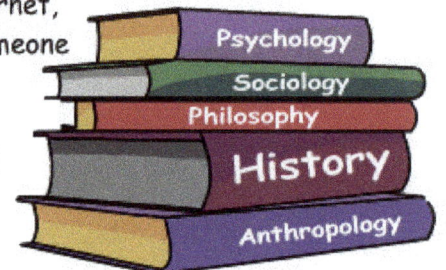

Use real-world references and focus more on man-made objects. Many designers are influenced by various sources. For example, if I like a color, I save it in my custom palettes. This is not about copying; it's about usingexisting elements for inspiration and adapting them to create something unique.

## MAXIMIZE CREATIVITY WITH LIMITED REFERENCES

Working with limited references is a key rule that helps you avoid distractions. Don't get confused or panic—mastery takes years of practice and continuous effort.

For example, if you're designing a train, research how many types of engines exist, gather as much information as possible, and then draw. When clients see this level of detail, they'll recognize you as a professional artist.

Remember: The goal is to learn how to draw a single object with many possible outcomes.

## Visual Memory

Designers use visual memory to draw from existing works, reference materials, or their own past creations. Students who draw correctly have a strong visual library. Those students who don't have a strong visual memory have a hard time.

## HOW TO MAKE VISUAL LIBRARY

There are two ways you can arrange your visual library.

**ONLINE RESOURCES**
(1) Design platform
(2) Social media.
(3) Stock websites
(4) Design blogs
(5) Game & Films
(6) Technology

**OFFLINE RESOURCES**
(1) Book
(2) Art galleries museums
(3) Nature walk
(4) Architecture
(5) Explore new places
(6) Travel & Experience

These are the things you feed your brain to generate good ideas, Things become more fun when you have a strong visual library. What you draw comes from your visual library. Some people read many books, which helps them create masterpieces and art that reflects culture. Drawing is a technical skill, but you also need to be good at the imaginative part so get good references and use them.

As a designer, plan a big trip every 1 or 2 years because photos never do justice to a place's energy, culture, or atmosphere. Each location has its own unique vibe. So, visit natural places and explore destinations that offer breathtaking views. Experience them firsthand to truly understand their essence. Nature is perfectly designed. Get inspiration from nature, as it offers the best forms and designs.

Note - Smell and sound are two things that actually serve as visuals to your brain.

Read books, this will help you create a variety of visuals and change the way you look at things.

# COMPOSITIONS

## Environment + Interior Design

The composition is designed to guide the viewer's eyes, making it more comfortable to observe and providing a more pleasant and effortless visual experience. Using composition, we can set priorities in an image while creating it and focus on the primary elements.

#1 Tip - Make the object look dissimilar when working with the environment. It's important to make objects stand out by making them look dissimilar from their surroundings. This can be achieved by contrasting the object with the environment in terms of color, shape, size, texture, or lighting. While adding micro details, make sure you do not distort the overall silhouette or composition of the drawing.

## WHEN SOMETHING MOVES FURTHER AWAY FROM YOU, MANY THINGS CHANGE.

- Intensity of light decreases.
- color information Go down.
- Intensity of light decreases.
- colour information Go down.

**They are separated.**

The fundamental rules cannot change. The more time you spend, the better you become at the technical aspects.

Tip- Add a creature or human to your environment design. This will help convey a story and make the design look more believable.

We can compress a world into a small location, establishing the world before establishing the architecture.

The first 5 minutes of your painting are always crucial because at this stage, you are defining the major forms, lighting, composition, and

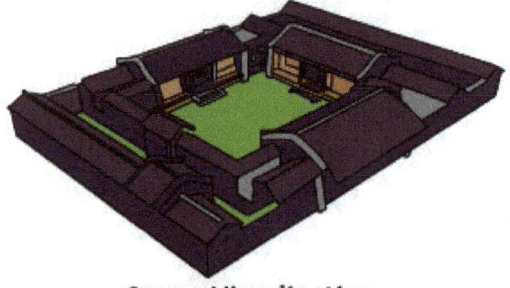

**Scene Visualisation**

perspective. Work in a way that you are comfortable with. Make sure your character belongs to your environment.

Always keep things simple. Don't approach design with unnecessary complexity. Add texture details that match your scene.

In entertainment, we can easily by pass logic to sell the design. Add dark-ness or light to areas to help identify key elements. Build things from the real world. Use culture to create a fantasy world.

## REAL-WORLD THINGS ARE EASY TO CONTROL

Using composition, we can control the pointof interest. When we say Amazon jungle, you think about the jungle, river, and trees, but we don't focus on every single detail; we catch glimpses of them now and then. So, we need to control the points of interest that we want the audience to see.

**Build things from the real world**

## FUNCTIONALITY

Interior spaces must be functional, and the artist must consider how the space would be used in real life. Depending on the style or era of the setting, the design of a space can reveal a lot about the character who inhabits it.

Design is all about solutions if your overdetails everything then every-things is died out.

## The Rule of Third

It involves dividing an image into nine equal parts using two equally spaced horizontal lines and two equally spaced vertical lines. These lines create a grid with nine sections. It is used in visual composition and is often applied in photography, painting, and design.

Audiences or viewers may not focus on rule or principle, but these elements are comfortable for the eyes and if you lose your camera you lose your composition.

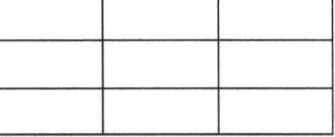
**Rule of third**

Once the rough drawing is done, start planning the camera shots and add more details than in the previous one.

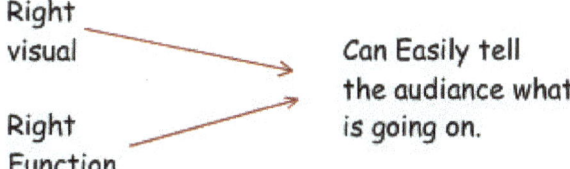

### THE RULE OF THIRD

Rule of Thirds improves artwork in the following ways :-

(1) It help to place main object of you composition along theseline or at the intersections.
(2) It creates a more balanced and harmonious composition.
(3) It helps guide the viewer's eye to important focal points.
(4) It adds interest by avoiding centering the subject.

Note
Most of the nature things are already balanced.

There is no shortcut, no special software, no filters, and no special brushes. The only things you have are time and practice. The more you practice these fundamental skills, the better you will become. It takes time to figure out what works in a particular project.

The large, giant creature serves as the main focal point, drawing the viewer's attention and guiding the composition's flow.

Balancing elements can help position our main subject off-center, allowing for negative space, which enhances the overall balance and harmony of the piece.

## THE RULE OF THIRDS PRINCIPAL IS USED FOR CREATING

(1) Illustration    (2) Photography    (3) Films & Video games
(4) Graphic Design    (5) Concept Art

Apply the Rule of Thirds in cartooning by creating a grid on your blank canvas before you start drawing. The next step is to identify the key elements of your drawing, such as the character, object, or background, and decide in which grid section each element fits best.

Placing important elements, like the character or key objects, at one of the four intersection points helps guide the viewer's eyes, making it easier to read the composition.

Grid Lines

Negative space                    Balanced composition

If you place an object on one side, add a secondary object on the opposite side to maintain balance.

Remember, this rule is not helpful in every design, so don't be afraid to break it. It totally depends on what you like and which part you want to balance your composition.

## Set Design

Set design refers to the process of designing and creating the backgrounds, environments, and locations where the characters and events take place. when working with films or video games, Set design is a very fun part. we never get bore as a designer the character is a small part of the overall design. The most important aspect is the set.

Add details to a scene according to the story. Identifying the light source in set design is a crucial part. Use bright colors, such as orange, to indicate the light source. Set design must be in correct proportions. It helps set up the overall mood of the composition.

The better you train yourself, the better you will draw. Industrial designers can sketch sets quickly because their job is to think and draw in 3D space or 3D perspective. As artists, we also need to develop this ability, even when creating cartoon backgrounds. make sure your design is presented in a presentable manner.

## FUNDEMENTALS

Primary Function - The set design is to create the visual environment that supports the narrative of the story. This starts with a good base, where we add details according to the story.

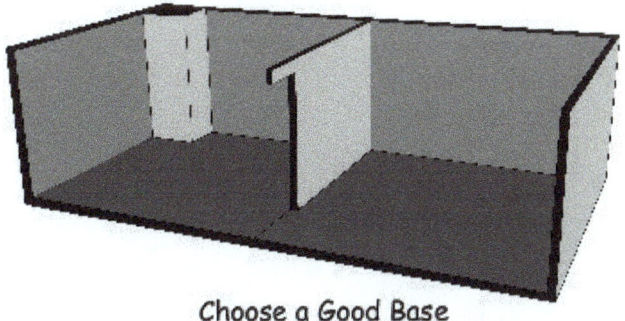

Choose a Good Base

For example, every game may have tables and chairs, but the overall feel and design of each game look different. This is where set design comes into play. We cannot build everything 100%; we have to decide which elements to capture based on the client's needs. People enjoy the experience by engaging with your set design.

Secondary Function - Secondary function supports the logistical, practical, and aesthetic needs of the Creation that complement the story without overwhelming it. In set design, the rules slightly change in the initial stage. There are no fundamentals at first; once we have the idea, we apply the fundamentals in the second drawings.

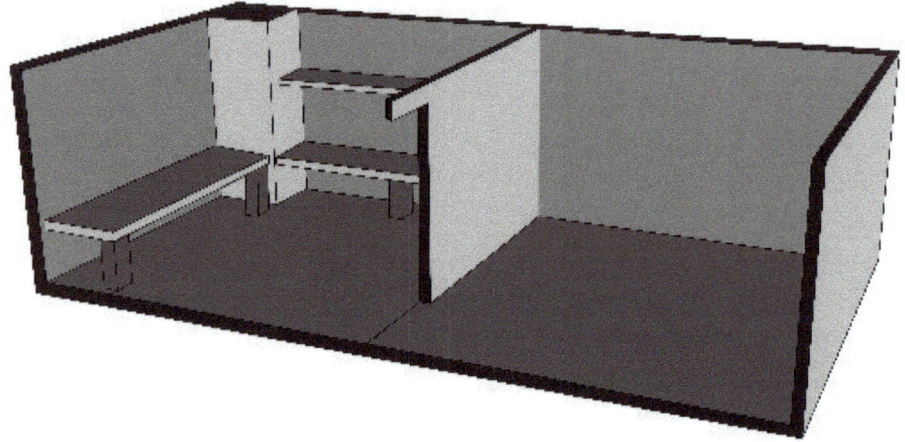

At this stage, introduce essential features.

Storytelling requires detailed planning, thinking, and problem-solving. The environments should belong to real-world themes, such as culture, history, science, and art. Focus on decreasing elements that cause stress and distractions. good results take the whole day, so don't try to compete with pros if you are a beginner.

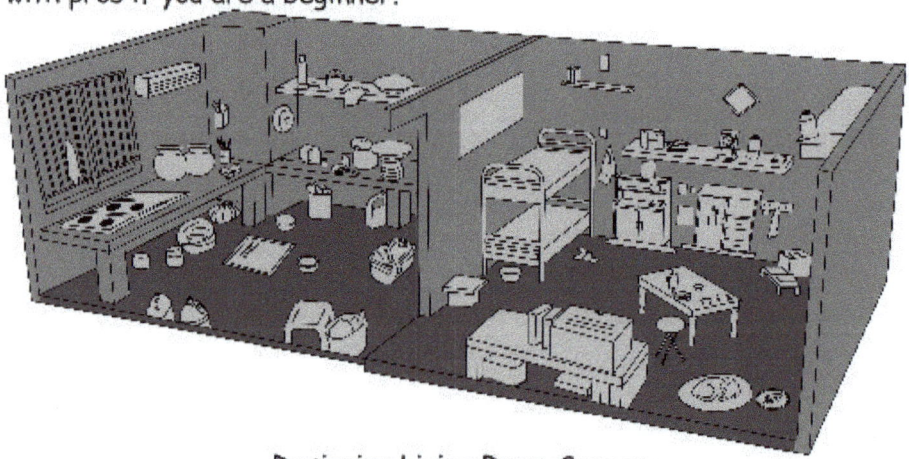

Designing Living Room Spaces

# C - 4   Colours Principal

### Colour Theory

Visual Design means creating appealing and effective designs using various principals & rules. colours communicate message and evoke emotions.

The color wheel illustrates the relationships between primary (red, blue, yellow), secondary (orange, green, purple), and tertiary colors. Primary colors are the foundation, secondary colors result from mixing two primaries, and tertiary colors are formed by combining a primary with a secondary color for example red + orange = fiery color.

A strong foundation allows you to push boundaries while maintaining clarity in your work. It helps you convey messages, communicate ideas clearly and effectively, and express emotions through visual elements. Understanding fundamental principles equips you with the tools to find creative solutions in various contexts.

A small color shift can change the overall feel of the composition

Think about how you present things. There are some artists who just paint, and their paintings look like photorealism because they understand the fundamentals and how color works.

## Colour knowledge

Understanding color psychology helps individuals and businesses communicate messages more effectively by using colors that evoke specific emotions and associations, influencing perceptions and behaviors in a targeted and impactful way.

## COLOR PSYCHOLOGY

**RED** - It represents love, passion, anger, strength, vitality, energy, and danger. Red is often associated with official or organizational settings, like the red carpet. It is commonly used in marketing to grab attention. Red is most frequently linked to love (e.g., Valentine's Day) and is also associated with energy.

**BLUE** - It represent Trust, clamness, stability, insperation and wisdom. it is mostly used in corporate branding to convey reliability (e.g., bank logos) and vehicle logos. Blue is also associated with technology. Blue is used by interior design to create a serene environments.

**GREEN** - It represents new beginnings, nature, growth, health, tranquility, peace, and good luck. Green is the traditional color of Islam and is associated with eco-friendliness and sustainability. It is commonly used in health-related branding and environmental campaigns.

**YELLOW** - It represents optimism, caution, positivity, and enlightenment, Yellow is associated with the mind and intellect and is used to evoke feelings of cheerfulness and energy. Yellow is effective in advertising because it attracts attention. Most YouTube thumbnails feature yellow text or highlights.

**ORANGE** - It represents creativity, vitality, enthusiasm, and warmth. It is popularly used in social media marketing to create a sense of urgency, especially in sales promotions.

**PURPLE** - It represents creativity, luxury, wisdom, and dignity. It is often used to convey a sense of elegance and sophistication and is commonly found in branding for high-end products or services. when we use purple in design it's very hard to balance the overall composition Purple is also associated with spirituality and mystery.

# Values

value refers to the lightness or darkness of a color. It plays a crucial role in creating contrast, depth, and emphasis within a design

Colors may differ, but they often share similar values. It's important to first understand and work with values before adding color. When working digitally, start by creating your painting in black and white, and then apply color later.

Light

Values are pleasing to the eye and should be categorized into light, medium, and dark. Be very careful when working with values, as even subtle changes can significantly affect the overall composition.

Dark

In illustration, it's crucial to work with values delicately and with attention to detail. If one value changes, it can impact other objects in the design.

Combination of Light and Dark

Higher value colors (lighter shades) tend to create a sense of airiness and openness, while lower value colors (darker shades) can evoke seriousness, sophistication, or depth.

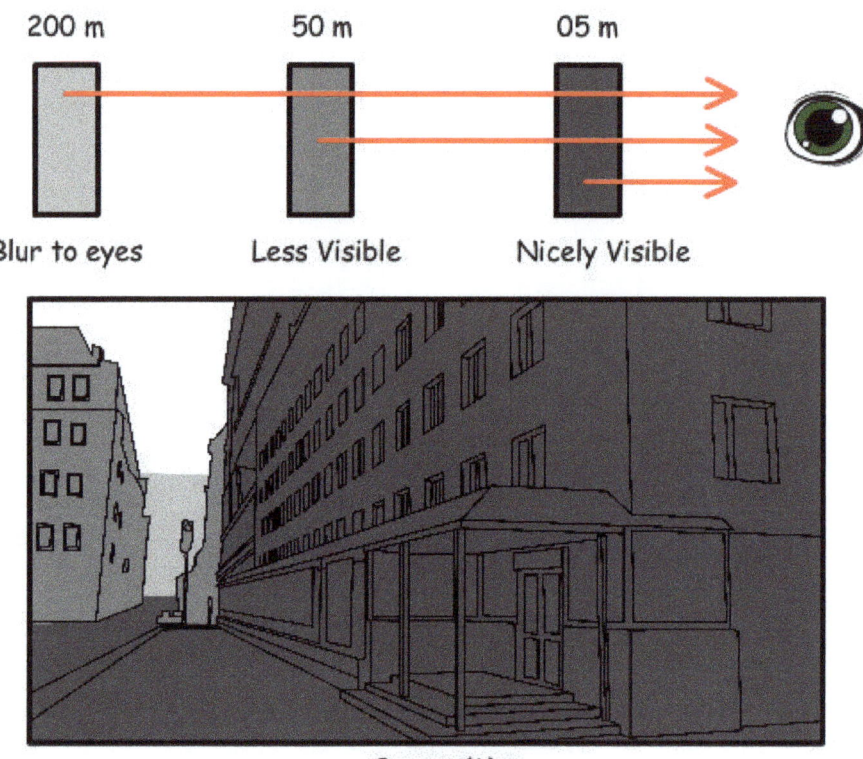

Composition

Most photographers beautifully use local values to highlight products, cars, and other items in commercials, enhancing their visual appeal.

Patience and confidence are important traits for a designer. as a designer demonstrates the effectiveness of value control in showcasing how well things are represented.

When there is an excess of white values, it becomes harder for the brain to identify objects clearly. A good pointer or technique is to break up silhouettes with varied values without causing distortion.

For example, cats and dogs have a slight reflection in their eyes, which helps them see in the dark. This reflection is different from ours, allowing them to have better night vision.

## Colour Balance

Color balance means choosing one main color, adding a few supporting colors, and using neutrals to make everything look good together.

The distribution should follow a certain ratio to create a balanced look. The 60-30-10 rule suggests using 60% dominant color, 30% secondary color, and 10% accent color to create a balanced and harmonious design with effective color distribution.

Purple, orange, and red are colors that can be difficult to balance. Sometimes, you have to trust your own best color combination to satisfy your client. So, don't be afraid to do this.

60 : 30 : 10
**PURPLE   YELLOW   BLUE**

This is a example of fantasy combination

Dominant color means picking one color that will stand out the most in your design. This color acts as the main focus and sets the tone for the rest of the design. Once you have the dominant color, you can add other colors later.

**Note**
In this business, visual work is important for us.

60 : 30 : 10
**YELLOW   BLUE   RED**

Light can make colors appear brighter, darker, or slightly different depending on where it's coming from. So, it's important to think about how light will affect the colors you choose, as it can make them look better or worse.

**Remember**
Make mistakes and learn how to fix those mistakes.

Play with the lightness and darkness of colors to create depth and focus.
Light colors make elements stand out, while darker tones add depth.

## SATURATION

Saturation defines color intensity, purity, and affects boldness or muteness. High saturation colors are vivid and impactful, while low saturation colors are muted, subtle, and evoke calmness, nostalgia, or a vintage feel.

This artwork consists of both high and low saturation.

## WARM VS COOL COLORS

Warm colors (reds, oranges, yellows) create energy and can bring elements forward, while cool colors (blues, greens, purples) tend to recede and create calm. A balance of both can prevent your design from feeling too intense or too flat.

Cool colors, such as blue, green, and purple, create a calming and relaxing atmosphere. These colors are linked to nature, water, and tranquility, making them ideal for designs aiming for peace and serenity.

Cool colour

Warm colors, like red, orange, and yellow, evoke energy, warmth, and excitement. They are associated with passion, enthusiasm, and activity, making them ideal for designs aiming to capture attention and create vibrancy.

Warm colour

## Balance composition

Balance composition means the arrangement of visual elements in an artwork, design, or photograph in a way that creates a sense of Balance. Different fields have different types of composition, each with its own set of guidelines and principles. Build confidence by learning from mistakes.

Use two colors in your painting so that the overall composition looks cohesive. While putting everything together, learn how to balance details. As designers, we need to simplify elements and create strong silhouettes. when working digitally, avoid relying on tricks and shortcuts. Don't depend on shortcuts without doing the necessary hard work.

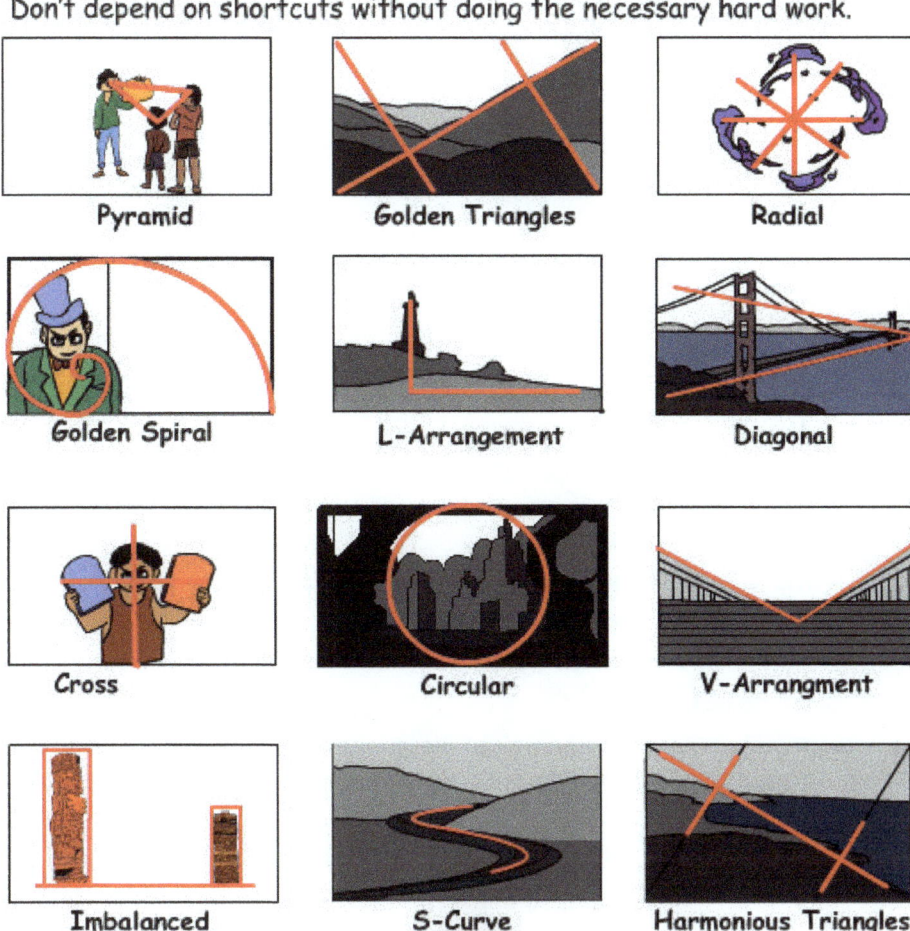

Pyramid — Golden Triangles — Radial

Golden Spiral — L-Arrangement — Diagonal

Cross — Circular — V-Arrangment

Imbalanced — S-Curve — Harmonious Triangles

## Light Reflection & Atmosphere

Light Reflection & Atmosphere means in design how light interacts with surfaces and how it influences the overall mood, depth, and perception of a design or artwork.

When you draw, it's important to learn how to light your scene effectively and understand how light interacts with the elements in it. Mastering light helps create depth, dimension, and realism in your artwork.

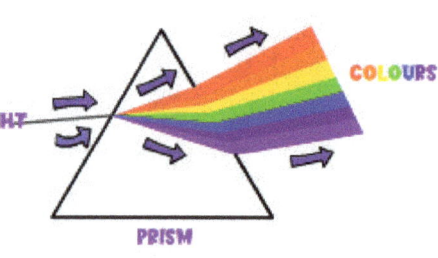

## LIGHT

**SOURCE**
Main light source

**PRIMARY**
Energy is converted into light

**SECONDARY**
Bounce or reflection of light

**EXAMPLES**
Sun

Light bubble, candle.

Bouncing board, surface, or anything that bounces.

## INTENSITY

How strong is the light source? We use value to define light in digital software. this helps a lot In a desert, the light hits the sand and causes it to shine. however, at night, the light is less visible, and fog creates a bounce effect. Always identify where the primary light source is coming from. In dark scenes, we work with lower intensity values to create the desired effect.

We see the world through light, Many students simply paint things out without fully understanding these concepts. These are basic fundamental mistakes.

Adding highlights to your character that blend with the background can significantly enhance the dramatic impact of your scene. The key is to have a strong, clear vision.

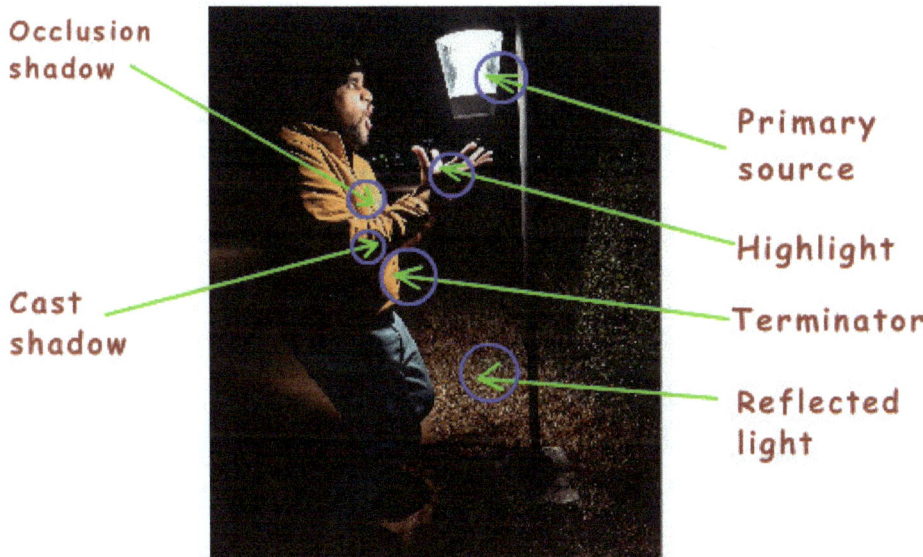

When light hits an object or human character in design, its behavior is influenced by surface properties, light intensity, and angle. Specular reflection occurs on smooth surfaces, creating sharp highlights, while diffuse reflection scatters light on rough surfaces, producing softer lighting. Shadows form where light is blocked, adding depth and volume. Highlights emphasize details and create realism, while specularity affects the glossiness of surfaces. Light absorption determines how dark or bright an object appears, with darker surfaces absorbing more light. Translucency allows light to pass through materials, creating subtle effects. The light angle further shapes the design's mood and depth.

When a tower acts as a light source, it illuminates surrounding areas, creating contrast, reflections, and highlights. The light's spread adds depth, drama, and atmosphere, influencing the scene's mood and perception.

As the distance between an observer and an object increases, the object appears blurrier due to the limitations of the eye's ability to focus. Light from distant objects spreads out more, reducing clarity. The lack of fine details and sharpness occurs because the eye's resolution decreases with distance.

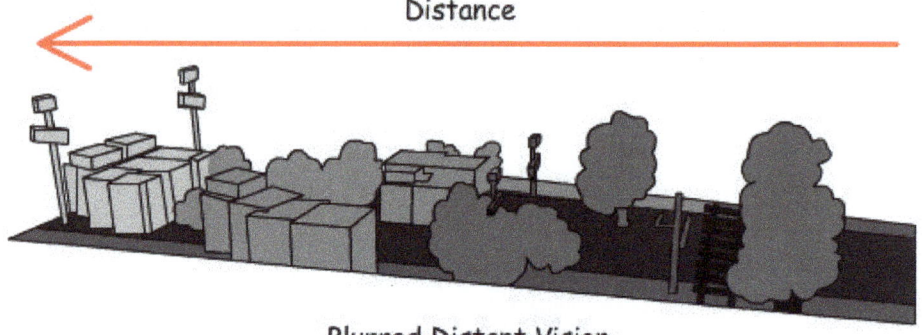

Blurred Distant Vision

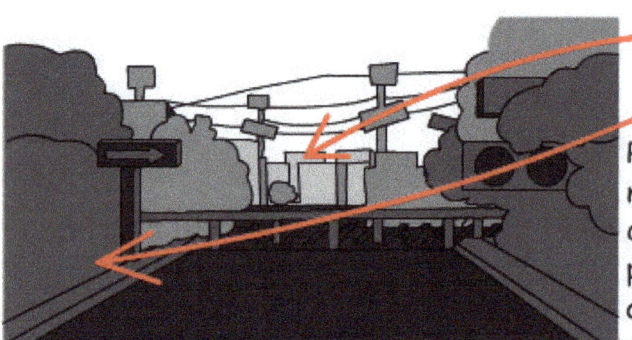

Far away

Close by

Placing a faraway object next to a nearby one creates depth through perspective. The closer object appears larger, while the distant one looks smaller and less detailed due to atmospheric effects

Particles or atmospheric effects create depth in a scene by adding layers and enhancing the sense of space. lighting intensities further enhance the sense of space and spatial relationships in the composition.

# Lighting and Values

The primary source of light is typically the sun or any light source that emits its own light, such as light bulbs or flames. It illuminates a scene directly, creating highlights and shadows. Secondary lights, like reflectors, are used to balance the lighting by filling in shadows and softening contrasts.

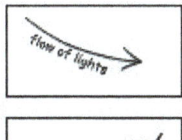

This is called flow of lights

The flow of light refers to how light travels from its source, interacting with objects by reflecting, refracting, or diffusing. It shapes highlights, shadows, and mood, influencing visual perception in a scene.

Fundamentals of lighting and how it impacts design and form in various lighting situations. Values are key; they help in implementing colors effectively. Most clients have a clear vision of the color tones they desire. Once values are properly balanced, the process becomes much easier.

Imagine light as a large bucket of water being poured onto a canvas. objects further away from you will appear lighter in value. Controlling light is crucial, as improper lighting can confuse the viewer. It's important to note that values, not colors, define the forms and shapes in a composition.

Values should be higher than the main elements, or vice versa, depending on the desired effect. What truly matters is the idea, feeling, and overall finish. Take it one step at a time, experimenting with different lighting scenarios. Remember, all designs go through an evolutionary process.

Note: First, values and volume must be balanced.

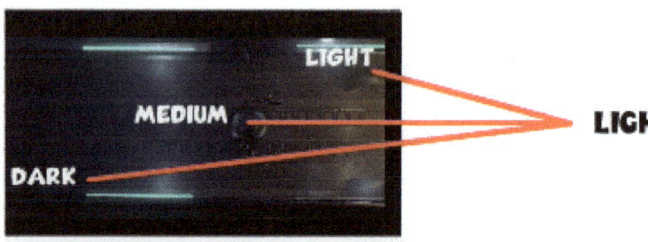

**LIGHT    MEDIUM    DARK**
This is how you stage your scene

Use local values to separate forms and shapes, creating clear distinctions between elements. Treat the set as if it's a real environment and apply virtual lighting accordingly. Ensure the subject matter is clean and visually appealing for the audience. Lighting plays a crucial role in making silhouettes stand out.

When working with values, you can adjust the colors later, especially when working digitally. Smartphone lights, which are microwave-based, are very weak and inadequate for proper lighting. Without a solid understanding of lighting fundamentals, the end result can appear dull and unappealing.

Poor distribution of light leads to bad composition.

Light should come from above, reflecting natural perception, with the sun or moon illuminating objects.

# Lighting Character

When light strikes a character, it influences their appearance by accentuating specific features and casting shadows.

## Colour pallets & Mood

Colour choices in cartoons evoke emotions, guide attention, and emphasize narrative elements. Warm colours (reds, yellows) suggest excitement or happiness, cool colours (blues, greens) convey calmness or mystery, while neutral tones (greys, browns) reflect seriousness. Bright colours indicate joy, and muted tones suggest melancholy or tension.

### 06 TO 07 AM COLOUR TONE
Colours for 6-7 AM include cool blues, purples, pastels, and muted tones to evoke calm, peaceful dawn light.

### 10 TO 12 AM COLOUR TONE
From 10 to 12 AM, bright, warm colours like yellows, oranges, and vivid blues create an energetic, lively atmosphere.

### 04 TO 06PM COLOUR TONE
From 4 to 6 PM, soft oranges, pinks, and golden yellows create a calming, peaceful atmosphere as day transitions.

### AFTER 09 PM COLOUR TONE
After 9 PM, deep blues, purples, and dark greys create a calm, restful atmosphere, while soft whites add warmth.

## LIGHT CONTRAST

They create visual interest and help elements stand out in design contrast colors draw attention, while low contrast creates a more subtle, harmonious effect.

## MOOD & COLOUR CONTRAST

Green is difficult to pinpoint in the traditional way because it occupies the center of the colour spectrum. Its appearance changes depending on the surrounding light sources, as well as the atmosphere. By combining these two factors, we can achieve the perfect formula for understanding its true nature.

By combining light and atmosphere, we get the perfect formula.

**LOCAL VALUES + LIGHTING ⟶ SILLOUTES**

Fog silloutes

Imbalanced composition

The most important thing is to balance the light. lighting in a scene enhances the subject without overpowering it.

Imbalanced Lights

Don't use too much light on objects g. Too much light can wash out details, flatten the composition.

When you observe nature, colors change due to the environment. For example, trees usually appear green in the normal season, but in winter, some trees appear blue.

## Stageing Character

The stage is the most important part. In the art industry, 40% of people know design, while the rest focus on rearranging objects to tell a story. If you are a designer, and you know how to draw from real life, have a visual library in your mind, and understand how to arrange objects in a specific way, then you have a designing job.

Know how basic things work and how to place them correctly so they appear natural. This technique is mostly used in films, but as an artist, we can also apply it.

 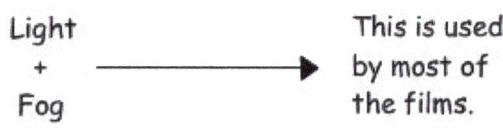

Light + Fog → This is used by most of the films.

These techniques to highlight characters or important objects. When there is more than one character on screen, their personalities must be defined to reflect their attitudes. Inconsistent staging would confuse the audience, making it unclear where to focus, which would distort the scene.

Staging is all about communicating effectively to your audience.

(1) Utilizing elements of layouts
(2) Background
(3) Composition
(4) Organization of character

## STAGING A TWO CHARACTER

Parallel angles                    Foreground profile

| Head Tops | Shoulder Frame | Mirror |

| Along Dividing Line | Through Crack | Through Grille |

| Through Crack | V/S characters | Negative Space |

Highlight the areas in your composition where you want your audience to focus. If you want to highlight a particular character among a crowd, a few things might help.

## STAGING THREE OR FOUR CHARACTERS

| Centred lineup | Foreground profile | Low Medium High Order |

 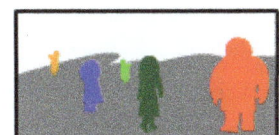 

| standing / seating | Group of people | Triangle |

| 4 corner/center | Head Torso 3/4 full | 1/2 panel profile |

# Approaching a Scene

First, the first 5 minutes of pointing are always crucial because, at this stage, you are defining major forms, lighting, composition, and perspective. Once we have this, we can focus on local details.

Now, start by understanding the subject matter. Create things that truly exist in your design, which requires proper planning and research.

**BEFORE APPROACHING A SCENE IDENIFY THIS ANSWERS 5 W'S**

1) What
2) Where
3) When
4) Who
5) Why

## WHAT (FUNDEMENTAL & TECHNICAL SKILL)

This means the fundamental artistic skills require style and visualgoals. What are you creating? What is the purpose of the scene or design? in cartoon creation or any visual design, this could include defining the major themes, characters, environments, and technicalaspects like color palette, texture, and composition.

## WHERE (EXTERIOR, INTERIOR & SCALE)

Where means the setting and environment. Where is the scene taking place? Is it indoors or outdoors? Urban or rural? The location influences the design elements such as lighting, perspective, background details, and the overall mood of the scene. Understanding the "where" helps to create a realistic or stylized environment that supports the narrative.

## WHEN (TIME PEROID APPROACH DETAIL)

When: The timing of the scene plays a role in the overall design. When does the scene take place? Is it day or night? A specific historical period or a futuristic setting? This will affect colours choices, lighting , and visual references (e.g., clothing, technology, architecture),which must align with the time frame to maintain consistency in the design.

## WHO (HUMAN EXPERIENCE ONCE INTERACTIVE DESIGN)

Who are the characters and how many characters are in the scene or elements involved in the scene? The design must reflect the traits, personalities, and roles of the characters or objects. This includes understanding the character's size, posture, expression, and how they interact with their environment. For cartoon creations, this often extends to exaggerating certain features to match the character's personality or function in the narrative.

## WHY (ENVIRONMENT VALUE & STORY ELEMENTS)

This is the most important question which you ask yourself self Why are you creating this scene? What is the purpose behind it? The "why" addresses the emotional tone, narrative purpose, and visual storytelling goal. Is it to evoke a particular emotion, create tension, or provide context for the story? The "why" helps drive design decisions, guidingeverything from composition to color choices, ensuring the design aligns with the intended message or mood.

Design Thinking

By answering the 5 W's—What, Where, When, Who, and Why you ensure that every design choice is purposeful and cohesive, enhancing the storytelling and emotional impact. This process might take some time but the result is worth it, create a scene that is not only visuallyengaging but also supports the overall message and tone of the narrative

The process of planning and conceptualizing how a scene or composition will be created. It involves considering various elements like:

## HAVE KNOWLEDGE OF THE CHARACTER

(1) What make the your character who is he.
(2) How Does he look at life.
(3) What are his basic attitude.
(4) How can you show what he is thinking and feeling through his movements ?
(5) What properties of drawing and movement makes you character unique to the other around them ?
(6) How old is your character.
(7) what are the Ground rule of your characters. you should never break them?

This process is challenging because it requires careful planning and lots of research. If you can convey the story of the scene in just a few drawings that communicate the key elements, you've already completed most of the work. Think like a comic strip artist, focusing on establishing attitude and poses. The great comic artists had the ability to encapsulate both attitude and action in a single pose.

## Presentations the things

Present multiple drawings on a single canvas, use a consistent layout with balanced spacing and a logical flow.

Use the same style across all the drawings to maintain a cohesive look. This includes line weight, color scheme, and overall tone to avoid jarring shifts between the images and Arrange the drawings in a way that tells a clear, logical story or progression the audience should be able to follow along effortlessly.

**Fill the blank spaces to complete your page.**

Use a Rough grid line on canvas to organize your drawings. Each panel can contain one drawing, andthe arrangement should guide the viewer's eye naturally across the sequence. The size, positioning, and spacing of each drawing should flow together cohesively.

Note
When you complete 10 to 20 thumbnails of a character or design, it's now fine to prepare for the presentation.

Have some line presenation while combining the design in one canvas. First, Understand why the client needs the character sheets. Are they for a game, a story, or a marketing campaign? after this go for detailed Breakdown of subject Go section by section through the character or object sheet, highlighting the important details.

# PRESENTING THINGS

## Ovation ETD-40

ETD-40 is a specialized LED lighting fixture used primarily in theatrical, broadcast, and live event environments.

Lightweight Design

Energy-efficient, long-lasting, and provide a consistent, bright output precise, gradual control over light intensity. consuming less power while still delivering a high output. Mounting options and can be easily integrated into different stage setups. suitable for use in environments where quiet operation is critical,

Quiet Operation

LED Technology

High-Quality Color Mixing

## Apply colour to Scenes

When designing, it's important to work in a way that feels comfortable for you, as the end result should always be satisfying. Every designer has their own unique perspective, problem-solving methods, and design language, which can evolve over time.

One key aspect of design is maintaining a consistent color scheme throughout the Scenes design. The colors should embody the character's personality, helping to visually communicate their traits. For example,

Warm Scenes

Cool Scenes

vibrant colors can indicate energy and enthusiasm, while muted tones may suggest introversion or melancholy.

Brights scene

Choose colors that evoke specific emotions aligned with the character's experiences or current state. A well-chosen color scheme can attract attention. establish Identity use colour to different the character from others.

Dark scene

A unique color scheme can help establish a strong visual identity, making the character memorable. While animating a scene, learn how colors can change over time as the character evolves, such as a shift from dark to bright colors.

## Apply colour to characters

This process involves several key steps that help bring the character to life and reflect their personality, story, and context. Utilize contrasting or matching colors, shadows, and highlights to add dimension, evolving colors as the character grows.

The main color of their clothing, hair, or skin. This should align with the character's Personality and there profession.

The main color of their clothing, hair, or skin. This should align with the character's Personality and there profession. colors can be used for small details, like , accessories, or highlights.

Highlights can add dimension

# C - 5  Design Strategy

## General Tips

Once you learn all the basic fundamental concepts, such as color theory, composition, perspective, and more, it's time for some tips and design strategies that you, as an artist, must keep in mind.

Knowing multiple art techniques is essential; if one doesn't work, you could be in trouble. Therefore, analyze the project and decide which technique will work best. Try different techniques, but ensure the end result looks good.

When you create work for clients, you shouldn't use that work in your portfolio or sell it if you're working in a studio, Always be honest with qyourself because nobody is watching you.

When you're working with clients, communicate as much as you can communication helps ensure that both you and your client have a clear understanding of the project's goals. Clients feel confident in your abilities when they see you're proactive in sharing updates.

Remember, Design goals for clients, not for yourself, High-paying clients are very busy people; they don't spend their whole day looking at your portfolio.

### BUILD A COMMON DESIGN LANGUAGE

Design language is used to create a consistent user experience across all platforms and products. It helps users recognize and connect with a brand by conveying its personality, values, and story.

Design involves combining elements in your own way, and you must cross the line of professionalism by practicing for many hours. Take mental breaks periodically, and then return to work.

Note - As designer you are also a Bussinessman.

## Freelance Tips

Every time you send a message to someone, don't feel the urge to overthink. It takes all of your creative energy. Just sit back and trust your work if your work is good, you no longer feel like you have to put on a mask when meeting clients and marketing yourself. In this bussiness you don't have to be in ego, you have to be very-very chill person.

Join supportive freelance community. Freelance tought me that building a business that works for you and choosing who you work with.

When you take on a bigger project, it can be difficult to process. Believe in yourself, and don't let anyone tell you that your dreams are too big.

"Freelancing offers the freedom to set your own rules and collaborate with the people you want to work with."

As a kid, one of my key special interests was art and design, and I am so grateful that people pay me for something I do for fun.

Create an achievement sheet for your own this will help keep you on track to work faster toward your goals.

### MAKE YOUR ACHIVEMENT SHEETS

| Achivement | Challenges |
|---|---|
|  |  |
|  |  |
|  |  |
|  |  |

Decide what is more important and what is less important. Make a list of everything you can think of that you will need to do to achieve each goal. If you list your achivements then it is easy for you to say motivated in bad days.

## LIST YOUR CLIENTS TO STAY CONNECTED WITH THEM

| Current / past clients | How to reach them with cold outreach ideas. |
|---|---|
|  |  |

## IDENTIFY THE MOST EFFECTIVE COLD OUTREACH STRATEGIES

| Create a package | How can I improve this package next year? |
|---|---|
|  |  |

Create design packages for clients; this will keep them accountable, Offer gold, silver, and bronze packages with prizes depending on the level.

## EARNINGS

| MONTHS | Current Year Earning | Next Year Earning Targets |
|---|---|---|
| January |  |  |
| February |  |  |
| March |  |  |
| April |  |  |
| May |  |  |
| June |  |  |
| July |  |  |
| August |  |  |
| September |  |  |
| October |  |  |
| November |  |  |
| December |  |  |

# Portfolio

Showcase high-quality work, include case studies which is done by you, and highlight your role in projects. Maintain a clean layout, update regularly, and add personal projects.

Your portfolio is 90% about your work and 10% about Your personality, so utilize both accordingly.

### REMEMBER
If you are a student you only show your good stuff.

"Present quality work, not quantity work" means showcasing your best projects instead of filling your portfolio with many mediocre ones. Quality highlights your expertise, engages clients with compelling stories, and differentiates you in a competitive field.

Five good pieces of artwork can go a long way in researching and planning your design.

| ART PORTFOLIO | V/S | DESIGN PORTFOLIO |
|---|---|---|
| One area is post-production, which deals with covers for magazines and covers for games. | | Another area is pre-production, which deals with sketch ideas related to your design portfolio. |

These two are different industries, but they intersect with each other. If your portfolio doesn't look professional, no one will give you projects. Some portfolios look bad due to a lack of fundamentals.

Build an online portfolio so companies can notice you. Sometimes, non experienced people are hired because of their portfolio. Some clients only want to see specific types of work. If you focus on a particular niche, it will be much easier for you to get a job.

Remember - Your design knowledge, fundamental skills, and passion are what make you a good designer.

The first point is that it's hard to find your design language. Once the design language is figured out, other things become easier. In studios, they look at portfolios before resumes; if the portfolio is strong, they then consider the resume.

It takes less than a minute to decide if you are good or not, and a few more minutes to decide if you are right for the job. So, make sure your portfolio stands out. In design, presenting well is key the design that is presented well always wins. Let the work speak for itself.

If every single image is different, it becomes hard to identify the strengths of this person, Always showcase your best work in your portfolio. if your work speaks for itself, people will find you.

Make everything available right away. If your portfolio doesn't look professional, no one will give you a project. Some portfolios look bad because they lack fundamentals. It's a professional career that may seem easy from the outside. Keep it simple. Fundamentals don't change; only the tools change.

## DEMONSTRATE PROBLEM-SOLVING SKILLS IN YOUR PORTFOLIO.

Describe the process, difficulties encountered, and how your solutions effectively addressed them. This shows your analytical thinking, creativity, and capability to apply design strategies. There are more design jobs available for those students who know about it. Develop the ability to solve design problems with limited things.

Designers with strong problem-solving skills are in high demand. By demonstrating your capability to address real-world design issues, you increase your chances of securing more diverse job opportunity.

## BAD PORTFOLIO

(1.) At first, Strong focus on technical skills instead of design.
(2.) Design becomes a form exercise, find an interesting form and render it.
(3.) Lack of strong elements (no story ) and after some time this student searches how to render stuff in 2 min.
(4.) Do the same things simply once you learn stuff every other thing is easy for you.

## Design solution for business

As an independent artist, it's crucial to stay updated on current trends, as this is a lifetime business that constantly evolves. As a designer, you have the ability to provide creative solutions. My role as a designer is to create something new—something that doesn't exist—and solve the client's problems, starting with a well-thought-out plan on paper. every artist needs a sketchbook because you should practice daily. Use a pen, as you need to draw things only once.

Research other artists to see what kind of achievements they have made and how they are earning. By doing this, you can combine your own strategy and start earning.

When practicing or working on client projects, set deadlines for yourself. Specialization comes with experience. In the beginning, you may need to work harder and more like a laborer, but over time, you'll be able to manage tasks more easily. Work hard so that clients seek you out, allowing you to earn a good income.

In design, the only thing that matters is the final result. As a designer, there is no single definition of design; whether it's 2D or 3D, your job doesn't change. You still need to create cool designs with a unique design language.

As a designer you have to Speak multiple design language adapting your style and approach to various projects, clients, and mediums, ensuring versatility and effective communication through design.

Things which you have to avoid there are several key elements you should avoid to ensure it presents you in the best light
(1) Fan art.
(2) No stick figers  most begginer artist do this in storyboard.
(3) Don't put practice work  on it.
(4) Don't copy design of other artist.
(5) Random work because client get confused what this person is doing.
(6) Irrelevant Work.

First, identify what your client wants. Understand whether your design style is illustration, industrial design, or concept art. Every artist has their own design language. Create options for clients so they can choose any of your designs.

Remember - A good package helps sell the product more.

When people don't have design ideas, they start buying things like 3D assets or brush packs. Instead, focus on design thinking.

When working with characters, present 5 to 6 characters on a single page, ensuring they are well-presented. All lines should connect seamlessly, without looking loose. Make sure that all your designs are original and not found on the internet; they must belong to you.

Take mental breaks when needed, but always return to your work with focus and determination.

If you're good at what you do, you can make a lot of money. Use your drawing skills to deliver effective solutions. In this industry, time is crucial. Many productions work under tight deadlines, so we must be able to work quickly and efficiently.

Use your elbow to draw, not your wrist. You have the ability to swing your elbow so things are made with flow.

Two things matter in the industry
(1) your portfolio.
(2) your personality (how cool you are).

Sometimes, when you ask a client what they want, they may not know. However, they are usually sure about what they don't want. When you know exactly what they want, you don't need to use too much imagination. If you work with the same client next time, you'll know what kind of design to avoid.

The purpose is not just to make a design beautiful; the purpose is to sell to the client. Every client appreciates details it's a key trick in business.

Note - Learn about money as soon as possible.

People hire designers for their unique design language. A good designer can see the extraordinary in ordinary things. In business, everything is controlled by deadlines. If you're a freelancer, the best way to advertise yourself is through your clients.

Note - It's bad for the business when you don't deliver things by the due date.

As a designer, first, draw everything. Later, focus on the parts you like the most. If you truly do good work and have someone else marketing for you, it's better than doing it yourself. When you produce excellent work, your name will travel to clients, or they will find you. sometimes, it's not always fun; it's work. After all, we are making a living from it

Anything that's worth money + worth time, without the headache is an = investment.

Clients are looking for things that help make or sell a product. Focus on the product and the technique.

### FIND A TRAINER & COACH THESE ARE TWO DISTINCT ROLES

(01) Once who trains the rules
(02) One who trains you to work with different scenarios.

The art industry is both fun and challenging. You have to work for days or months, and it can take years to produce something. The hardest part is creating something new from existing ideas. We are not just paid for our designs; we are paid for our time.

Remember - Art is a process, but the end result is showcasing a design.

### Pipeline

The difference between the illustrator and designer industries is that, while both use drawing to communicate ideas, their career paths are very different from each other.

## ILLISTRATION

Artist ---- > Artwork ---- consumer

Artwork = Money

(01) Artwork is money.
(02) Illustration is done for books.
(03) The end result is artwork, created purely to sell the product.
(04) Individual.
(05) Personal style.
(06) Heavy focus on anatomy and figures.
(07) Freedom to experiment.
(08) Self-promotion.
(09) Book covers,
(09) movie covers.

## DESIGN INDUSTRY

(01) The main focus is not on artwork but the product.
(02) The consumer never see the artwork behind how create this
(03) Focus mainly on entertainment design
(04) Common workflow
(05) Industry techniques
(06) More focus on problem solving and design
(07) Work in pipleline
(08) Mass consumer focused
(09) We make things for large amount of audience.
(10) Mostly focus on entertainment
(11) Example Games, industry ect.

Sometimes, two different career paths meet with similar interests. For example, the Transformers movies are made by industrial designers, but marketing teams create toys and take help from illustrators.

Industrial designers are seen by developers, as they provide the foundation for the development process. The developer acts as the pipeline, bringing designs to life. For designers, artistic style accounts for 10%, while production and functionality make up 90%. Different variation drawings help explore multiple design possibilities and solutions.

Illustration is designed with the audience in mind, as they are the ones who purchase the work. For book covers, graphic designers prioritize aesthetics and effective communication. In illustration, the emphasis is on crafting a product with clear expression, solid forms, and compelling single images that engage viewers.

## Things to Avoid

If you want to become a professional artist then you must avoid this things.

1) Playing long hours of video games. Just for reference gathering, instead, watch gaming videos. The prerecorded games have a very nice visual library.

2) Fan art - This doesn't teach you because you are looking at someone else's design, These things are not good for students who are studying. Don't use other people's photoplates. Stop looking at other people's work for references, because there is a higher chance you'll end up copying their art. Try creating your own and gather your own resources. Get your own things.

3) Not using real-world references - As a pro, use as many references as you can because you can't memorize everything. References are used by most industrial artists.

4) Immature content - Your content must be mature and appealing to clients. Our job is to solve the client's problems, not create more problems for them.

5) Don't show references to clients - Gathering references takes a lot of time, but it doesn't solve the design problem or provide a design solution. Clients aren't looking to wait for days while you gather reference images.

## REMEMBER

If you are a student, focus on one thing at a time to make the situation easier for yourself, especially when you're learning.

This happened in my early days: Clients would ask me to finish a design, and from the first day, I didn't have any designs ready. The next day, I got nervous, and by the end of the day, I lost the project. This is the story of my first 2D animation music video.

## Clients need and clients want!

Underpromise and overdeliver. Focus on solving your clients' problems rather than creating more. Use positive marketing and work with people or clients you enjoy collaborating with. When a client gives you a job, do exactly what they ask for, without overdoing it. Don't push yourself to work under pressure, such as trying to finish a design in less than 30 minutes—especially if you're a student. This approach is for professionals.

Try to present multiple ideas, not just one. The moreideas you present, the higher the chances your design will be selected. What clients primarily want from you are ideas and designs. Even rejected designs can help refine your concepts. It's important to have a strong understanding of the client's background to create original and marketable designs.

## If you work with multiple clients, ...

Have a manager, if you can handle multiple projects at a time. A producer can manage your company's cash flow, decide where to allocate money, and protect you from the business side, allowing you to focus on the design aspect.

Clients only want the final design that belongs to you. Identify the key pieces in your portfolio that work for you. Work with those who understand your design language quickly. Details should be finalized after the design is approved. Remember, Be a designer who prioritizes the client first. We are giving choices to the clients, we are not here to make drawings, we are here to create products. If you provide only one drawing, you don't give the client a choice. If they don't like that one image, the conversation stops.

We are not making art we are making products. We're not creating art for its own purpose; we're designing functional products that address specific needs, solve problems, and deliver value to clients and users in a practical, meaningful way.

Every solution comes with validation, making each project enjoyable. Some projects are highly skill-demanding as you're designing solutions. Clients often don't understand how many hours you spend on a design, they only want the final piece. Feel free to explain that the artwork involves a significant amount of time and effort, which justifies the price you charge time and effort are directly tied to the value of your work.

# CLIENT-CENTRIC DESIGN STRATEGIES.

In freelancing, we work on commission and are paid based on time there is no luxury. Never put your clients second; this is a business, not just creating artwork. As designers, our first goal is to understand the client's needs. Clients prefer to work with professionals. They are buying the idea, not the techniques. Sometimes, you may need to sacrifice your own preferences to make the client happy. Clients want well-designed work, and often within a short timeframe.

They don't care about your techniques. clients may not care about the techniques behind your work, explaining your process briefly can help them appreciate the value and effort involved in creating the design. Speed is important but never sacrifice the quality of your work. Clients appreciate work that is both thought-fully designed and well-executed, So time clients may might like idea but make not like the design.

**Clients & Designers**

As designers, we need to understand the market and what clients want. When I first talk to a client, I ask two things:
(1) The client's needs.
(2) The client's budget.

Success as designers comes from understanding trends, client needs, and expectations. Clients provide us with design direction, which helps ensure the final design aligns with their vision and meets their expectations.

# DESIGN SOLUTION

The design solution you provide to your clients is 90% based on their needs, with the remaining 10% reflecting your unique input, which makes the design great.

## 90% SIMILAR  10% NEW
### CLIENT SAFE

The design solution you provide to your clients is 50% based on their requirements, with the other 50% showcasing your creativity and fresh perspective.

## 50% SIMILAR  50% NEW
### RISKY SIDE

This design solution provide to your clients is 30% based on their specifications, with 70% being your innovative ideas and creativity, Mostly your vision.

## 30% SIMILAR  70% NEW
### DANGEROUS SIDE

we create a small percentage of the actual artwork; it's more of a mental game. New designs should incorporate familiar elements to make them relatable and appealing to clients.

If you show variations to clients, then
(1) Your first design must be a safe design.
(2) The second design may be generated or a mixture of more creative elements.

Clients want consistent

## REJECTION

Rejection is a part of the process. We create many things, and many are rejected, so love your work. what one client or audience may not connect with, another may love. Every project is a learning experience, helping you better understand client preferences, market demands, and your own creative boundaries. The fear of rejection leads to underpricing your services.

## PROCRASTINATION

Procrastination is a result of avoiding something you don't want to do. Procrastinating on work means you're not enjoying it. When I'm working, I get completely immersed and forget to eat.

Have a clear art direction. Many clients may say one thing today and something completely different tomorrow, and after a few days, they may even quit the project. That's why it's crucial to have a strong art direction in place.

## GLOBAL BIG GOAL IS TO SOLVE A PROBLEM.

Clients always seek pros, and these are the individuals who truly control the industry, where most clients turn to. The whole point is to communicate the idea. If the client is happy with it, we can add details later. Most beginner artists try to avoid the difficult tasks and aim to make their work look like that of pros.

TIPS - When working with clients, there is no room for experimentation due to deadlines it's best to play it safe. Drawing is a small part of the business, we are selling an idea.

### POINT TO NOTED

Don't come off as desperate; carry yourself with confidence. Why are you so desperate to get a job if your work is that good? Instead, have confidence. Clients may take advantage of you by offering lower rates, so always maintain your confidence.

## ESTIMATE YOUR WORK

Clients

Once you know your target hourly rate, it doesn't mean you must always charge that amount. There will be times when you can charge more, but you should never charge less.

The Question is how you decide your hourly rate. Here are few step and simple mathematical calculation through this you can easily calculate your hourly rate.

Step 1 ) If you are doing a job, what salary would you be happy with, considering your expertise and the industry?

STEP 2) Now, the main part: You have 52 weeks in a year. Remove 4 weeks for annual leave, leaving you with 48 working weeks.

For Example, suppose your annual salary is 1 lakh INR

Here some calculation part.
You have 52 weeks in a year, minus 4 weeks for annual leave, leaving 48 working weeks.

Divide 1 lakhs with 48 (weeks)
1,00,000 /48 = **2,083**
**2,083** is your weekly income

Now divide 2,083 by 6 (your have 6 working days)
2,083 / 6 = **347.5** (this is your daily income)

Now divide 347.5 with 7 because you have 7 hour working sedule
347.5 / 7 = **57.8**
Congratulations, you've got your hourly rate, which is **57.8 RS**. Your minimum hourly rate helps you achieve the salary you want. But remember, as a freelancer, if you purchase specific software or a template for a client, make sure to add these costs to your hourly rate.

## ASK QUESTION TO CLIENTS

These are the two questions you should ask your clients to get better design solutions.
Q.1) In your business, which area is struggling or where your clients tend to get stuck and ask many questions?
Q.2) Please list the things you expect from clients regarding the project, so that you and your clients can collaborate effectively moving forward. These questions may vary depending on the client and the specific service package they've purchased.

> Learn every detail of your business. If you become very good at what you do, nothing can stop you from getting paid more and being promoted faster.- Dan Kennedy

## GROW YOUR MONEY MINDSET

Unlock your money mindset and expand your thinking to realize what is possible for you and your business. By setting clear boundaries around your time, money, and energy, you will boost your confidence and be able to raise your prices. Write down your business processes and don't be afraid to make mistakes — they happen when your mind is racing or you forget key steps. Once you identify these challenges, refining your processes will lead to increased efficiency and success.

Once it's done, you can focus on tasks that generate revenue and invest your energy into growing your business by optimizing your time and resources.

Consider these few questions to ask yourself before setting a price for your project.

(01) Is the deadline soon?
(02) How big is the client
(03) Is there someone else readily available who could do the work? For example, your design charge is $200, but you could probably charge $600 if the client needs it by tomorrow.

The top 5 percent of Americans see themselves as self-employed, no matter who signs their paychecks. As a legend once said, 'When you start doing what you truly love, you'll never work another day in your life.

Financial success is the result of doing certain specific things over and over again until you achieve the financial independence you desire. The law of cause and effect states that if you do what other successful people do, you will eventually get the results that other successful people get. And if you don't, you won't.

# TWO QUESTIONS TO UNLOCK YOUR DREAMS

Q1 ) What is one thing I would dare to dream if I knew I could not fail?
   Dreaming big is the starting point of achievement.
Answer _____
_____
_____

Q2 ) If you won the lottery today, would you continue doing what you are currently doing?
Answer _____

Last Tip - Begin each goal with the word 'I' to Feel it personal to you.

Create a Daily Design Exercises that move you at least one step closer to your financial independence goal, Remember nobody is better than you, and nobody is smarter than you.

## THANKS

Dear Readers,

As you reach the final pages of "The Art of Cartooning Anything," I want to take a moment to express my heartfelt gratitude to every one of you. Thank you for embarking on this creative journey with me. Your passion for exploring the whimsical world of cartoon design fills me with joy and inspiration.

This book was crafted with the hope that it would ignite a spark of creativity within you, regardless of your age Whether you're a budding artist or someone who simply wishes to express their imagination, I hopeyou found encouragement and guidance in these pages. Remember, creativity doesn't have boundaries. , and it resides within all of us, waiting to be unleashed. I hope this book has empowered you to pick up your pencil, embrace your unique style, and bring your ideas to life through cartooning. Your creations have the power to bring smiles, so never hesitate to share your artistic voice with the world.

Thank you for your support, your enthusiasm, and your commitment to exploring the art of cartooning. May your creative journey continue to flourish, and may you always find joy in the process of bringing your imagination to life.

Sending my best wishes
Himanshu Mire